"MY NAME IS ETHAN ALLEN"

A LITTLE MAID
OF
TICONDEROGA

BY

ALICE TURNER CURTIS

AUTHOR OF

A LITTLE MAID OF OLD NEW YORK
A LITTLE MAID OF OLD PHILADELPHIA
A LITTLE MAID OF MASSACHUSETTS COLONY
A LITTLE MAID OF OLD CONNECTICUT
A LITTLE MAID OF PROVINCETOWN
A LITTLE MAID OF MARYLAND

ILLUSTRATED BY WUANITA SMITH

APPLEWOOD BOOKS
BEDFORD, MASSACHUSETTS

A Little Maid of Ticonderoga was first published by the Penn Publishing Company in 1917.

ISBN 1-55709-330-X

Thank you for purchasing an Applewood Book.
Applewood reprints America's lively classics—
books from the past that are still of interest to modern readers.
For a free copy of our current catalog, write to:
Applewood Books, P.O. Box 365, Bedford, MA 01730.

10 9 8 7 6 5 4 3

Printed and bound in Canada.

Library of Congress Cataloging-in-Publication Data
Curtis, Alice Turner.
    A little maid of Ticonderoga / by Alice Turner Curtis;
illustrated by Wuanita Smith.
        p.   cm.
    Summary: While visiting her aunt and cousin near Fort
Ticonderoga, Faith Carew learns a secret about the fort that
concerns Ethan Allen's "Green Mountain boys."
    ISBN 1-55709-330-X
    1. United States—History—Revolution, 1775–1783—
Juvenile fiction.   [1. United States—History—Revolution,
1775–1783—Fiction.   2. Vermont—Fiction.]
I. Smith, Wuanita, ill.   II. Title
PZ7.C941Lmt   1996
[Fic]–dc20   96-28379
                                          CIP
                                          AC

Introduction

THIS is the story of a little girl whose home was among the Green Mountains of Vermont, then known as "The Wilderness," at the beginning of the American Revolution; and at the time when Ethan Allen and his brave soldiers were on guard to defend their rights. Ethan Allen was the friend of Faith, the heroine of the story, whose earnest wish to be of help is fulfilled. She journeys from her Wilderness home across Lake Champlain to Ticonderoga, and spends a winter with her aunt and cousin near Fort Ticonderoga. Here she learns a secret about the fort that is of importance later to Ethan Allen's "Green Mountain Boys."

There are two very interesting bears in this story. Like the other volumes of this series, *A Little Maid of Old New York*, *A Little Maid of Old Philadelphia*, *A Little Maid of Old Connecticut*, *A Little Maid of Provincetown*, *A Little Maid of Massachusetts Colony*, and *A Little Maid of Maryland*, the present volume introduces the heroes of American history and tells of famous deeds and places of which all American children should know.

3

Contents

A Little Maid of Ticonderoga

CHAPTER I

ESTHER AND BRUIN

FAITH CAREW was ten years old when Esther
Eldridge came to visit her. Faith lived in a big comfortable log cabin on one of the sloping hillsides of
the Green Mountains. Below the cabin was her
father's mill; and to Faith it always seemed as if the
mill-stream had a gay little song of its own. She
always listened for it when she awoke each morning.

"I wonder if Esther will hear what the brook
sings?" thought Faith as she drew on her moccasin
slippers and dressed as quickly as she could, for her
mother had already called her twice, and Faith had
just reached the top of the stairs when the third call
of, "Faith! Faith! I shall not keep your porridge hot
another instant," sounded from the kitchen.

"I'm coming, mother dear," the little girl called
back, and hurried down the stairs, wondering to herself why grown people who could always do exactly
as they pleased should think it best to rise before the
sun was really up.

"Your father was off to the mill an hour ago," said
Mrs. Carew, setting a bowl of steaming porridge on

the end of the table beside a narrow window, "so you will have to eat your porridge alone."

Faith sat down at the table, looking out through the open window toward the mill.

"I do hope Esther Eldridge and her father will come to-day," she said. "Do you think they will, mother dear?"

"Yes, child; they will probably arrive before sunset. Your father expected them yesterday. It will be a fine thing for you to have a little girl for a companion. But she is a village child, and may not be happy in the Wilderness," responded Mrs. Carew.

"Why, of course she will like being here! Just think, she has never seen wheat ground into flour! And she can see that in our mill; and she has always walked on real roads, and here she will not even see a road; and I know many pleasant paths where we can walk, and I can tell her the names of different trees and flowers. I'm sure she will think the Wilderness a fine place," said Faith, nodding her head so that her yellow curls seemed to dance about her face.

"I hope they make the journey from Brandon safely. Your father has been told that the Indians have been troublesome to the settlers near Lake Dunmore; and besides that, there are many bears coming out into the clearings these fine autumn days. But Mr. Eldridge is a good shot, and I am seeking trouble in naming Indians or bears. Finish your breakfast, Faithie, and run to the garden and bring me in the ripest of the pumpkins; for I must make some cakes for our company."

The Carews lived in a log house on a slope of cleared ground running down to the mill-stream. There were no roads, only rough trails, and they had no near neighbors. Faith's father had a large grant of land, a "New Hampshire Grant," it was called, which ran toward the eastern shore of Lake Champlain. Faith had no playmates, and when Mr. Eldridge, of the town of Brandon, had sent word that he was coming to see Mr. Carew on business and would bring his small daughter with him, Faith had been overjoyed and had made many plans of what she would do to entertain her visitor.

Faith finished her breakfast, and helped her mother clear the table and wash the dishes, and then went up the slope to where a number of fine pumpkins and squashes, growing among the corn, were ripening in the early September sunshine. She looked about carefully, and selected a yellow pumpkin. "This is about as large as my head," she said aloud, "and I guess it is about the same color," and she ran back to the house carrying the pumpkin, which Mrs. Carew set to bake in the brick oven beside the fireplace.

"When it is baked may I fix the shell for a work-basket for Esther?" asked Faith.

"Yes, indeed," answered Mrs. Carew smilingly. "Your Aunt Prissy was greatly pleased with the one you gave her when she visited here last autumn."

"I wish I could go to Ticonderoga and visit Aunt Prissy," said Faith.

"Why, so you shall some day. But 'tis a troublesome journey, since one must be set across the strait," replied her mother. "But look, child! Can it be that Mr. Eldridge has arrived at this early hour?"

"Yes, indeed. I see his little girl! Look, mother! Father has lifted her down from the horse; and Mr. Eldridge is walking, too! Oh, mother! See the fine hat she has on!" and Faith ran to the open door to get a better look at the little girl who was walking so slowly up the path to the log house.

In a moment the little girl looked up toward the open door and Faith waved her hand.

"She didn't wave back, mother dear," exclaimed Faith, and then the travelers were close at hand, and Mrs. Carew was greeting the tall, grave-faced man and welcoming Esther.

"My little girl was so tired that we stopped for the night at your neighbor Stanley's house, five miles east," said Mr. Eldridge; "and that is why we are in good season this morning."

While Mr. Eldridge was speaking Esther held fast to her father's hand, her large black eyes fixed on Mrs. Carew. Faith looked at her admiringly, wishing that her own eyes were black, and that her feet were small like Esther's, and that she had a hat with a wide scarlet ribbon.

"Esther, this is Faith," she heard her mother say, "and she will try and make you so happy here that you will wish to stay all winter."

The two little girls smiled shyly, and Esther let go her clasp on her father's hand and followed Mrs. Carew into the pleasant kitchen. Faith watched her eagerly; she wondered why Esther looked about the big room with such a curious expression. "Almost as if she did not like it," thought Faith.

The little gray kitten came bouncing out from behind the big wood-box and Esther gave a startled exclamation.

"It's just 'Bounce,'" said Faith, picking up the kitten and smoothing its pretty head. "I named it 'Bounce' because it never seems to walk. It just bounces along."

Esther smiled again, but she did not speak. Faith noticed that she was very thin, and that her hands looked almost like little brown shadows.

"Are you tired?" she asked, suddenly remembering that she had heard her father say that "Mr. Eldridge's little maid was not well, and he thought the change would do her good."

Esther nodded. "Yes, I'm always tired," she answered, sitting down in the low wooden rocker beside the light stand.

"For pity's sake, child, we must see to it that you are soon as strong and well as Faith," said Mrs. Carew, untying the broad scarlet ribbon and taking off Esther's hat. She smoothed back the dark hair with a tender hand, remembering that Esther's own mother was not well, and resolving to do her best for this delicate child.

"I think the pumpkin is cooked by this time, Faithie. I'll set it in the window to cool and then you can take out the pulp and I'll make the cakes," said Mrs. Carew.

Bounce jumped up in Esther's lap, and Faith sat down on the braided rug beside her.

"I'm going to make the pumpkin shell into a work-basket for you," said Faith. "Did you ever see a pumpkin-shell work-basket?"

Esther shook her head. She did not seem much interested. But she asked eagerly: "Are the pumpkin cakes sweet?"

"Yes, indeed. You shall have one as soon as they are baked; may she not, mother dear?"

"Why, yes; only if Esther is not well it may not be wise for her to eat between meals," responded Mrs. Carew.

"Oh! But I eat cakes whenever I want them," declared Esther, "and I love sweets. I had a fine cake when I left home and I ate it all before we got to Lake Dunmore."

Mrs. Carew thought to herself that she did not wonder Esther was always tired and not strong. Esther did not say that the "fine cake" had been sent as a gift to Faith. But her face flushed a little, and she added, "I meant to bring the cake as a present; but I was hungry."

"Of course you were," agreed Faith quickly. "Is not the pumpkin cool enough to cut, mother dear?" asked Faith.

"Yes," replied her mother, setting the yellow pumpkin on the table.

"Come and see me do it, Esther," said Faith, and Esther, with a little sigh, left the comfortable chair and came and leaned against the table.

With a sharp knife Faith cut a circle about the stem of the pumpkin and took it off, a little round, with the stem in the center. "That will be the work-box cover," she explained, laying it carefully on a wooden plate. Then she removed the seeds and the pulp, putting the pulp in a big yellow bowl, and scraping the inside of the pumpkin shell. "There! Now when it dries a bit 'twill be a fine work-box, aid it is for you, Esther," she said; but Esther was watching Mrs. Carew, who was beating up eggs with the pumpkin pulp.

"Do you put spices in the cakes?" she questioned eagerly. "How long before they will be baked?"

Faith stood holding the yellow pumpkin shell, and looking at her visitor wonderingly.

"All she cares about is something to eat," thought Faith, a little scornfully, setting the fine pumpkin shell on the table.

Esther's face brightened as she listened to Mrs. Carew's description of pumpkin cakes, and of pumpkin pies sweetened with maple syrup.

"I think I must teach you to cook, Esther. I am sure you would soon learn," said Mrs. Carew.

"I guess I wouldn't be strong enough," responded Esther in a listless tone, going back to the rocking-chair, without even a glance at Faith's present.

"Come, Esther, let's go down to the mill. I'll show you the big wheel, and how father raises the water-gate," suggested Faith, who was beginning to think that a visitor was not such a delightful thing, after all.

Esther left her chair with a regretful sigh, and followed Faith out-of-doors.

"Listen!" said Faith. "That rippling, singing noise is the brook."

Esther laughed. "You're funny," she said. "Why should I listen to a noisy old mill-stream?"

"I thought perhaps you'd like to hear it. I do. Sometimes, just as I go to sleep, I hear it singing about the stars, and about little foxes who come down to drink, and about birds—" Faith stopped suddenly, for Esther was laughing; and as Faith turned to look at her she realized that Esther cared nothing about the music of the stream.

"I do believe you are silly," Esther responded. "Do you think your mother will bake the cakes and pies while we are away?"

"Yes," replied Faith dully. Only that morning she had said to herself how nice it would be to have a girl friend to talk with, but if Esther thought she was "silly"—why, of course, she must not talk. "I'll let her talk," resolved Faith.

For a few moments the two little girls walked on in silence, then Esther said suddenly: "Does your mother ever let you boil down maple molasses for candy?"

"Sometimes," replied Faith.

Esther slipped her little brown hand under Faith's arm. "Ask her to let us make candy this afternoon.

Do. Tell her it will keep me from being lonesome. For my father will be going to Ticonderoga as soon as dinner is over; he will be gone for days. Will you ask her, Faith?"

"Yes, I'll ask her," Faith answered.

"I know I'm going to have a fine visit," declared Esther, with more interest than she had shown since her arrival. "Does your mother ever bake little pies, in saucers, for you?"

"No," said Faith, still resolved to say no more than was necessary.

"Oh! Doesn't she? That's too bad. I wish I had asked her to. Then we could play keep-house in the afternoon, and have the pies to eat? Will your mother make pies again to-morrow?"

"I don't know," said Faith.

Esther did not care much about the mill. She hardly glanced at the big water-wheel, and was eager to get back to the house. Several times she reminded Faith of her promise about the maple candy. Faith had expected that she and Esther would be the best of friends, but the time before dinner seemed very long to both the children.

Soon after dinner Mr. Eldridge went on his way. He left his horse in Mr. Carew's care, as he was to walk to the shore of Lake Champlain and trust to good fortune to find a canoe or boat in which he could cross the narrow strait to Ticonderoga. He would not return for a week, and he seemed greatly pleased that his little daughter was so contented to be left with her new friends.

"She is an only child, like your own little maid," he said to Mrs. Carew, "and I am glad they are to be friends."

They all walked down the slope with him, and watched him striding off along the rough path.

"He's going to fetch me some rock-candy," said Esther as they turned back to the house.

Mrs. Carew stopped at the mill, and the two little girls went back to the house.

"We'll make the maple candy now, shan't we?" said Esther, as they reached the kitchen door. "See, the kettle is all clean, and I know where the molasses jug is," and before Faith could remind her that she had not yet asked permission, Esther was dragging the heavy jug from the pantry.

"Oh, look out, Esther. You'll spill it," cautioned Faith, running to help her.

"No, I won't. Here, help me turn it into the kettle and get it over the fire before your mother comes back," urged Esther, and the two girls lifted the jug and turned the maple syrup into the kettle. "There, that will make a lot of candy," said Esther. "You stir up the fire and put on more wood."

Faith obeyed. She hardly knew what else she could do, although she was sure that her mother would not want them to use all the syrup for candy. As she piled on the wood, she heard a scrambling noise at the door, and a sudden scream from Esther: "Faith! Faith! A bear! A bear!" and looking over her shoulder she saw a big brown bear coming in through the kitchen door.

CHAPTER II

FAITH MAKES A PROMISE

FOR a second Faith was too frightened to move. Then pulling one of the newly kindled sticks from the fire she hurled it at the big creature and ran for the stairs, up which Esther was already hurrying.

The flaming brand halted the bear for a second only, but the little girls had reached the upper floor before he was well into the kitchen, and, sniffing the molasses, he turned toward the empty jug and the full kettle.

"What shall we do? What shall we do?" sobbed Esther. "He will come up here and eat us. I know he will."

"We must get out of the window and run to the mill," whispered Faith. "We mustn't wait a minute, for mother dear may be on her way to the house. Come," and she pushed Esther before her toward the window. "Here, just take hold and swing yourself down," she said.

"I can't, oh, I can't," sobbed Esther.

"You must. I'll go first, then;" and in a moment Faith was swinging from the window-sill, had dropped to the ground, and was speeding down the path to the mill, while Esther, frightened and helpless, leaned out screaming at the top of her voice.

Mrs. Carew was just leaving the mill when she saw Faith racing toward her. "A bear! A bear in our kitchen," she called.

"Hugh!" called Mrs. Carew, and Mr. Carew came running from the mill to hear the story.

"It's lucky I keep a musket at the mill," he said. "Here, you take Faith into the mill and fasten the door on the inside. I'll attend to the bear," and he was off, racing toward the house, while Mrs. Carew hurried Faith into the mill and shut the heavy door.

"I do hope Esther will stay in the chamber until your father gets there," said Mrs. Carew anxiously. "I do not believe the bear will venture up the stairs."

"He was after the syrup," said Faith, "and if he tried the stairs Esther could drop out of the window."

It was not long before they heard the loud report of the musket.

"Mayn't we open the door now, mother dear?" asked Faith.

"Not yet, Faithie. We'll wait a little," and Faith realized that her mother's arm trembled as she drew the girl to her side.

There was silence for what seemed a very long time to Mrs. Carew and Faith, and then they heard Mr.

Carew calling, "All right, open the door. Here is Esther safe and sound."

Esther, sobbing and trembling, clung to Mrs. Carew, and Faith held tight to her father's hand while he told the story. The bear, with his nose in the kettle of syrup, had not even heard Mr. Carew's approach, and had been an easy mark.

"You'll find your kitchen in a sad state, Lucy," said Mr. Carew, as he finished. "I have dragged the bear outside, and he will furnish us some fine steaks, and a good skin for a rug; but your kettle of syrup is all over the floor."

"Kettle of syrup?" questioned Mrs. Carew. "Why, there was no kettle of syrup." Neither of the little girls offered any explanation. Mr. Carew looked about the clearing to see if any other bear was in the neighborhood, but it was evident that the creature had come alone.

" 'Tis not often they are so bold," said Mr. Carew, as they neared the cabin, "although last year an old bear and two cubs came down by the mill, but they were off before I could get a shot at them."

Mrs. Carew looked about her kitchen with a little feeling of dismay. The kettle had been overturned, and what syrup the bear had not eaten was smeared over the hearth and floor. The little rocking-chair was tipped over and broken, and everything was in disorder.

Esther looked into the kitchen, but Mrs. Carew cautioned her not to enter. "You and Faith go to the front door and go into the sitting-room," she said. "There is nothing that either of you can do to help;" so Faith led the way and pushed open the heavy door which led directly into a big comfortable room. The lower floor of the cabin was divided into two rooms, the sitting-room and kitchen, and over these were two comfortable chambers. The stairs led up from the kitchen.

Faith thought the sitting-room a very fine place. There was a big fireplace on one side of the room, and the walls were ceiled, or paneled, with pine boards. On one side of the fireplace was a broad wooden settle, covered with a number of fur robes, and several big cushions. Between the two front windows stood a table of dark wood, and on the table were two tall brass candlesticks. A small narrow gilt-framed mirror hung over the table.

There were several strongly-made comfortable wooden chairs with cushions. The floor was of pine, like the ceiled walls, and was now a golden brown in color. There were several bearskin rugs on the floor, for Mr. Carew, like all men of the "Wilderness," was a hunter; and when not busy in his mill or garden was off in the woods after deer, or wild partridge, or larger game, as these fine skins proved.

"What a funny room," exclaimed Esther, with a little giggle. "Our sitting-room has beautiful paper on the walls, and we have pictures, and a fine carpet on the floor. What are you going to tell your mother about that maple syrup?" she concluded sharply.

"I don't know," responded Faith.

"Well, don't tell her anything," suggested Esther.

"I guess that I shall have to tell her," said Faith.

"You mean about me? That I teased you to make candy? Well, if you do that I'll get my father to take me home with him instead of staying until he comes next month," declared Esther.

"I shan't tell anything about you," answered Faith.

Esther looked at her a little doubtfully.

"Of course I shan't," repeated Faith. "You are my company. No matter what you did I wouldn't talk about it. Why, even the Indians treat visitors politely, and give them the best they have, and that's what I shall do," and Faith stood very straight and looked at Esther very seriously.

"Truly? Truly? What is the 'best' you have? And when will you give it to me?" demanded Esther, coming close to her and clasping her arm. "Is it beads? Oh! I do hope it is beads! And you can't back out after what you have said," and Esther jumped up and down in delight at the thought of a possible string of fine beads.

For a moment it seemed as if Faith would burst into tears. She had meant to tell Esther that she would do her best to be kind and polite to her because Esther was a guest, and now Esther was demanding that Faith should do exactly as she had promised and give her "the best she had." And it happened that Faith's dearest possession was a string of fine beads. Aunt Priscilla Scott, who lived in Ticonderoga, had brought them as a gift on her last visit. They were beautiful blue beads,—like the sky on a June day,—and Faith wore them only on Sundays. They were in a pretty little wooden box in the sitting-room closet.

Suddenly Esther let go of Faith's arm. "I knew you didn't mean it," she said scornfully.

Faith made no reply. She walked across the room and pushed a brass knob set in one of the panels. The panel opened, and there was a closet. The little wooden box that held the beads was on the middle shelf. Faith took it up, closed the door, and turned toward Esther.

"Here! This is the best thing I have in all the world, the prettiest and the dearest. And it is beads. Take them," and she thrust the box into Esther's eager hands and ran out of the room. She forgot the dead bear, the wasted syrup, the danger and fright of so short a time ago; all she could think of was to get away from Esther Eldridge.

She ran across the clearing and along a narrow path that circled behind the mill into the woods. She ran on and on until she could no longer hear the sound of the brook, and the path began to grow rocky and difficult. Then, tired and almost breathless, Faith sat down on a big rock and looked about her. For a few moments she could think of nothing but her lost beads, and of the disagreeable visitor. Then gradually she realized that she had never before been so far along this rough path. All about her rose huge, towering pines. Looking ahead the path seemed to end in a dense thicket. She heard the rustle of some little forest animal as it moved through the vines behind her, and the call of birds near at hand. Faith began to recall the happenings of the morning: the excitement of Esther's arrival, the sudden appearance of the bear in the kitchen doorway, her terror lest her mother should come before she could be warned; and then, again, Esther and the loss of her beads. She began to cry. She felt very tired and unhappy. She felt Esther was to blame for everything, even for the appearance of the bear. Never before had a bear dared come to the house. Faith leaned back against a friendly tree with a tired little sigh. She would rest, and then go home, she thought, and closed her eyes.

When she awoke, she thought she must still be dreaming; for, standing a little way down the path, was a tall man leaning on a musket. He wore a flannel blouse, and his homespun trousers were tucked into high leathern gaiters.

The man smiled and nodded. "Do not be frightened, little maid," he said in a friendly voice. "I did not want to leave you here in the woods until I was sure that you could make your way home. Are you Miller Carew's little girl?"

"Yes, sir," answered Faith, wondering who this tall, dark-eyed man, who knew her father, could be, and then adding, "My name is Faith."

The tall man smiled again, and took off his leather cap.

"My name is Ethan Allen," he responded; "it may be that you have heard your father speak of me."

"Yes, sir! You are a Green Mountain Boy; and you help the settlers to keep their 'Grants,'" Faith replied quickly; for she had often heard her father and mother speak of the trouble the settlers were having to prove their titles to land taken under the "New Hampshire Grants," and she remembered hearing her father say that Ethan Allen would help any man defend his rights. She wished that she could tell him all about Esther Eldridge and the blue beads, but she remembered her promise. "I guess there are times when people don't have any rights," she decided, and was quite unconscious that she had spoken aloud until she heard her companion say very clearly:

"There can never be such a time as that. People would be slaves indeed not to uphold their just and rightful claims. But why is a small maid like yourself troubling about 'rights'?"

"I have company at my house—" began Faith.

"I see, I see!" interrupted Colonel Allen. "Of course you have to let the guest do whatever she pleases," and he smiled and nodded, as if he understood all about it. "And now we had best start toward your father's mill, for it is well toward sunset."

"Sunset? Have I slept all the afternoon!" exclaimed Faith, jumping up.

As they walked down the path Ethan Allen asked Faith many questions about the people who came along the trail from the settlements on their way to Lake Champlain.

When they reached the clearing where the mill stood Faith's father and mother came running to meet them. They welcomed Mr. Allen, and said that they had been sadly worried about Faith. "But where is Esther?" asked Mrs. Carew. "Is she not with you, Faith?"

"I left her in the sitting-room, hours ago!" answered the little girl.

CHAPTER III

MORE MISCHIEF

"'Hours ago,'" repeated Mrs. Carew. "Why, dear child, it is only an hour since Esther came up from the mill with the dishes."

Faith looked so bewildered that her mother exclaimed: "Why, child! Have you forgotten that you and Esther had your dinner at the mill?"

"But I did not have any dinner," declared Faith. "It was not dinner time when I ran off and left Esther in the sitting-room. I—" and then Faith stopped suddenly. She resolved that she would not tell her mother that she had given Esther the blue beads,—not until Esther was found.

"Well, I declare. Esther came into the kitchen just as I was preparing dinner, and asked if you girls could not have a picnic dinner at the mill, and I was well pleased to let you. I put some cold meat and bread, a good half of pumpkin pie and some of the pumpkin cakes in a basket, and gave her a pitcher of milk, and off she went. An hour ago she came in to ask for a lunch and I gave her a good piece of molasses cake. Your father was busy skinning the bear, and we gave but little thought to you children. But when I called your name, and found neither of you at the mill, I became alarmed. But where can Esther be now?" concluded Mrs. Carew, looking anxiously about the clearing.

"Go back to the house with Faith and give the child something to eat. Colonel Allen and I will search the mill again," said Mr. Carew.

"I'm tired," said Faith, as they reached the house, "and I don't like Esther."

"Hush, Faithie. She is your guest. And if she has wandered into any harm or danger I do not know what we can say to Mr. Eldridge," responded her mother; "but I do not understand about the food," she added, half to herself, wondering if Esther could really have eaten it all.

Faith looked about the kitchen. "It looks just the same. Just as if the bear had not come in," she said.

Mrs. Carew brought her a bowl of milk and a plate of corn bread, and another plate with two of the pumpkin cakes.

"I'll run back to the mill while you eat your supper, Faithie, and see if Esther has been found. When I come back you must tell me what you were turning syrup into the kettle for."

Faith was hungry, but as she ate her bread and milk she felt very unhappy. She remembered her promise to Esther not to tell Mrs. Carew about the syrup.

"I don't know what I shall do," she said aloud. "I guess I'll go and rest on the settle until mother dear comes," so she opened the door and entered the sitting-room. As she lay back among the cushions of the settle she heard a faint noise from the further side of the room. "I guess it's 'Bounce,'" she thought.

Then the noise came again: "Gr-r-r! Gr-rrr!" Faith sat up quickly. She wondered if another bear had made its way into the house. The big black bearskin rug in front of the table was moving; it was standing up, and coming toward the settle.

"It's you, Esther Eldridge! You can't frighten me," said Faith, and Esther dropped the rug from her shoulders and came running toward the settle. Her black eyes were dancing, and she was laughing.

"Oh! I've had the greatest fun! I ate all your dinner, and I hid under that bearskin and your mother and father hunted everywhere for me. Where have you been?" concluded Esther, looking down at Faith. The little girls did not notice that, just as Esther began speaking, Mrs. Carew had opened the sitting-room door.

"I've been way off in the woods, and my mother has asked me to tell her about the maple syrup," replied Faith accusingly.

"Well, Esther!"

Both the girls gave an exclamation of surprise at the sound of Mrs. Carew's voice. "You may go to the mill and tell Mr. Carew that you are safe, and then come directly back," she said a little sternly, and stood by the door until Esther was on her way. Then she crossed over to the settle and sat down beside Faith.

"I will not ask you about the syrup, Faithie dear," she said, smoothing Faith's ruffled hair. "And you had best go up-stairs to bed. I will have a talk with Esther, and then she will go to bed. It has been a difficult day, has it not, child? But to-morrow I trust everything will go pleasantly, without bears or trouble of any sort."

"But Esther will be here," said Faith.

"Never mind; I think Esther has made mischief enough to-day to last all her visit," responded Mrs. Carew; and Faith, very tired, and greatly comforted, went up to her pleasant chamber which Esther was to share. She wondered to herself just what her mother would say to Esther. But she did not stay long awake, and when Esther came up-stairs shortly after, very quietly, and feeling rather ashamed of herself after listening to Mrs. Carew, Faith was fast asleep.

But Esther did not go to sleep. She wondered to herself what her father would say if Mrs. Carew told

him of her mischief, and began to wish that she had
not deceived Mrs. Carew about the dinner. She could
feel her face flush in the darkness when she remembered what Mrs. Carew had said to her about truth-
fulness. Esther's head ached, and she felt as if she
was going to be ill. Down-stairs she could hear the
murmur of voices. Ethan Allen would sleep on the
settle, and be off at all early hour the next morning.
It seemed a long time before the voices ceased, and
she heard Mr. and Mrs. Carew come up the stairs.
Esther began to wish that she had not eaten the fine
pumpkin pie and all the cakes. It was nearly morning
before she fell asleep, and she was awake when Faith
first opened her eyes.

"It's time to get up. It always is the minute I wake
up," said Faith sleepily.

Esther answered with a sudden moan: "I can't get
up. I'm sick," she whispered.

Faith sat up in bed and looked at Esther a little
doubtfully. But Esther's flushed face and the dark
shadows under her eyes proved that she spoke the
truth.

"I'll tell mother. Don't cry, Esther. Mother will
make you well before you know it," said Faith, quickly slipping out of bed and running into the little passage at the head of the stairs.

In a few moments Mrs. Carew was standing beside the bed. She said to herself that she did not wonder that Esther was ill. But while Faith dressed and got ready for breakfast Mrs. Carew smoothed out the tumbled bed, freshened the pillows and comforted their little visitor.

"Run down and eat your porridge, Faithie, and then come back and sit with Esther," said Mrs. Carew.

When Faith returned Mrs. Carew went down and brewed some bitter herbs and brought the tea for Esther to drink. The little girl swallowed the unpleasant drink, and shortly after was sound asleep. She had not awakened at dinner time, and Mrs. Carew was sure that she would sleep off her illness.

"The child must be taught not to crave sweet foods," she said, as she told Faith to run down to the mill and amuse herself as she pleased. "Only don't go out of sight of the mill, Faithie," she cautioned, and Faith promised and ran happily off down the path. She was eager to ask her father about Mr. Ethan Allen.

Mr. Carew was busy grinding wheat. There were few mills in the Wilderness, and nearly every day until midwinter settlers were coming and going from the mill, bringing bags of wheat or corn on horseback over the rough trail and carrying back flour or meal. When Mr. Carew had tied up the bag of meal and his customer had ridden away, he came to where Faith was sitting close by the open door and sat down beside her.

"Why do you call Mr. Allen a 'Green Mountain Boy'?" asked the little girl, after she had answered his questions about Esther; "he is a big man."

Mr. Carew smiled down at Faith's eager face, and then pointed to the green wooded hills beyond the clearing. "It's because he, and other men of these parts, are like those green hills,—strong, and sufficient to themselves," he answered. "Every settler in the Wilderness knows that Ethan Allen will help them protect their homes; and no man knows this part of the country better than Colonel Allen."

"Why do you call him 'Colonel'?" asked Faith.

"Because the Bennington people have given him that title, and put him in command of the men of the town that they may be of service to defend it in case King George's men come over from New York," replied her father; "but I do not know but the bears are as dangerous as the 'Yorkers.' Do you think Esther will be quite well to-morrow?" concluded Mr. Carew.

Faith was quite sure that Esther would soon be as well as ever. She did not want to talk about Esther.

She wanted to hear more about her friend Colonel Allen. "I heard him tell mother that he slept in a cave one night on his way here," she said.

"Oh, yes; he can sleep anywhere. But you must talk of him no more to-day, Faithie," answered Mr. Carew; "and here is 'Bounce' looking for you," he added, as the little gray kitten jumped into Faith's lap.

CHAPTER IV

A NEW PLAN

ESTHER was much better the next morning, but she was not well enough to come downstairs for several days, and when her father appeared he agreed with Mrs. Carew that the little girl was not fit to undertake the journey on horseback along the rough trail to Brandon.

Mrs. Carew was able to assure him, however, that he need not be anxious about his little daughter, and he decided to go directly home, leaving Esther to regain health and strength in Mrs. Carew's charge.

"I will come for you the first Monday in October, three weeks from to-day," he told Esther, "and you must mind Mrs. Carew in everything she bids you."

Esther promised tearfully. She did not want to stay, but she resolved to herself, as she watched her father ride away, that she would do everything possible to please Mrs. Carew and make friends with Faith. She could hardly bear to think of the first day of her visit.

As she lay on the settle comfortably bolstered up with the soft pillows, and a little fire crackling on the hearth, Esther looked about the sitting-room and began to think it a very pleasant place. Faith brought all her treasures to entertain her little visitor. Chief of these was a fine book called "Pilgrim's Progress," with many pictures. There was a doll,— one that Faith's Aunt Priscilla had brought her from New York. This doll was a very wonderful creature. She wore a blue flounced satin dress, and the dress had real buttons, buttons of gilt; and the doll wore a beautiful bonnet.

Faith watched Esther a little anxiously as she allowed her to take Lady Amy, as the doll was named. But Esther was as careful as Faith herself, and declared that she did not believe any little girl that side of Bennington had such a beautiful doll.

"I think your Aunt Priscilla is the best aunt that ever was. She gave you this lovely doll, and your blue beads—" Esther stopped suddenly. She had lost the beads, and she did not want to tell Faith. She had resolved to hunt for them as soon as possible, and give them back. She was sure she could find them when she could run about again.

Faith did not look at Esther. She wished Esther had not reminded her of the beads. But Esther had been so grateful for everything that Mrs. Carew and Faith did for her that they had almost forgotten her mischief, and were beginning to like their little visitor.

"Yes, my Aunt Prissy is lovely," said Faith. "She is a young aunt. Her hair is yellow and her eyes are blue; she can run as fast as I can," and Faith smiled, remembering the good times she always had when Aunt Prissy came for a visit to the log cabin. "When I go to visit her I shall see the fort where the English soldiers are," she added.

"Colonel Ethan Allen could take the fort away from them if he wanted to; my father said so," boasted Esther; and Faith was quite ready to agree to this, for it seemed to her that the tall, dark-eyed colonel could accomplish almost anything.

"How would you and Faithie like to have your supper here by the fire?" asked Mrs. Carew, coming in from the kitchen. "Faith can bring in the light stand and use her own set of dishes. And I will make you a fine dish of cream toast."

Both the little girls were delighted at the plan. And Faith ran to the kitchen and, with her mother's help, brought in the stand and put it down in front of the settle. She spread a white cloth over it, and then turned to the closet, from which she had taken the blue beads, and brought out her treasured tea-set. There was a round-bodied, squatty teapot with a high handle, a small pitcher, a round sugarbowl, two cups and saucers, and two plates. The dishes were of delicate cream-tinted china covered with crimson roses and delicate buds and faint green leaves.

One by one Faith brought these treasures to the little table, smiling with delight at Esther's exclamations of admiration.

"My grandmother who lives in Connecticut sent me these for my last birthday present," said Faith. "My Grandmother Carew, whom I have never seen. And they came from across the big salt ocean, from England."

"To think that a little girl in a log cabin should have such lovely things!" exclaimed Esther. "I have a silver mug with my name on it," she added.

Mrs. Carew brought them in the fine dish of cream toast, and filled the china teapot with milk so they could play that it was a real tea-party. There were baked apples to eat with the toast, and although Esther longed for cake she did not speak of it, and, bolstered up with cushions, and Faith sitting in a high-backed chair facing her, she began really to enjoy herself.

"My father made this little table," said Faith, helping Esther to a second cup of "tea," "and he made these chairs and the settle. He came up here with Mr. Stanley years ago, and cut down trees and built this house and the barn and the mill; then he went way back where my grandmother lives and brought my mother here. Some day I am to go to Connecticut and go to school."

"Why don't you come to Brandon and go to school?" suggested Esther. "Oh, do! Faith, ask your mother to let you go home with me and go to school this winter. That would be splendid!" And Esther sat up so quickly that she nearly tipped over her cup and saucer.

"I guess I couldn't," replied Faith. "My mother would be lonesome."

But Esther thought it would be a fine idea; and while Faith carried the dishes to the kitchen, washed them with the greatest care, and replaced them on the closet shelf, Esther talked of all the attractions of living in a village and going to school with other little girls.

"I feel as well as ever," declared Esther as the two little girls went to bed that night; "but l do wish your mother thought sweet things would be good for me. At home I have all I want."

"Mother says that is the reason you are not well," answered Faith. "Hear the brook, Esther! Doesn't it sound as if it was saying, 'Hurry to bed! Hurry to bed!' And in the morning it is 'Time to get up! Time to get up!'"

"You are the queerest girl I ever knew. The idea that a brook could say anything," replied Esther;

but her tone was friendly. "I suppose it's because you live way off here in the woods. Now if you lived in a village—"

"I don't want to live in a village if it will stop my hearing what the brook says. And I can tell you what the robins say to the young robins; and what little foxes tell their mothers; and I know how the beavers build their homes under water," declared Faith, with a little laugh at Esther's puzzled expression.

"Tell me about the beavers," said Esther, as they snuggled down in the big feather-bed.

"Every house a beaver builds has two doors," began Faith, "and it has an up-stairs and down-stairs. One of the doors to the beaver's house opens on the land side, so that they can get out and get their dinners; and the other opens under the water— way down deep, below where ice freezes."

"How do you know?" questioned Esther, a little doubtfully.

"Father told me. And I have seen their houses over in the mill meadow, where the brook is as wide as this whole clearing."

Before Faith had finished her story of how beavers could cut down trees with their sharp teeth, and of the dams they built across streams, Esther was fast asleep.

Faith lay awake thinking over all that Esther had said about school; about seeing little girls and boys of her own age, and of games and parties. Then with a little sigh of content she whispered to herself: "I guess I'd be lonesome without father and mother and the brook."

Mrs. Carew had heard Esther's suggestion about Faith going to Brandon to go to school, and after the little girls had gone to bed she spoke of it to Faith's father, as they sat together before the fire.

"Perhaps we ought to send Faithie where she could go to school and be with other children," said Mr. Carew, "but I hardly know how we could spare her."

There was a little silence, for the father and mother knew that their pleasant home on the slope of the hillside would be a very different place without their little maid.

"But of course we would not think of Brandon," continued Faith's father. "If we must let her go, why, her Aunt Priscilla will give her a warm welcome and take good care of the child; and the school at Ticonderoga is doubtless a good one."

"Esther seems sorry for her mischief, but I should not wish Faith to be with her so far from home. Perhaps we had best send some word to Priscilla by the next traveler who goes that way, and ask her if Faith may go to her for the winter months," said Mrs. Carew.

So, while Faith described the beaver's home to the sleepy Esther, it was settled that as soon as it could be arranged she should go to stay with her Aunt Priscilla in the village of Ticonderoga, across Lake Champlain, and go to school.

"If 'twere not that some stray Indians might happen along and make a bonfire of our house and mill we might plan for a month's visit ourselves," said Mr. Carew.

"We must not think of it," responded his wife. For the log cabin home was very dear to her, and at that time the Indians, often incited by the British in command of the forts at Ticonderoga and Crown Point, burned the homes of settlers who held their land through grants given by the New Hampshire government.

"More settlers are coming into this region every year. We shall soon have neighbors near at hand, and can have a school and church," said Mr. Carew hopefully. "Colonel Allen is not journeying through the wilderness for pleasure. He has some plan in mind to make this region more secure for all of us. Well, tell Faithie, if she has aught to say of going to Brandon, that she is soon to visit Aunt Priscilla. I doubt not 'twill be best for the child."

CHAPTER V

ESTHER did not find the blue beads; and when her father came for her she had not said a word to Faith about them.

Mr. Eldridge found his little daughter fully recovered from her illness, and in better health than when she came to the Wilderness. When she said good-bye Faith was really sorry to have her go, but she wondered a little that Esther made no mention of the beads, for Esther had been a model visitor since her illness. She had told Mrs. Carew the full story of the attempt to make maple candy, which the bear had interrupted, and she had claimed the pumpkin-shell work-box with evident delight. All these things had made Faith confident that Esther would return the beads before starting for home, and she was sadly disappointed to have Esther depart without a word about them.

Esther had asked Mrs. Carew if Faith might not go to Brandon, and so Mrs. Carew had told the little girls of the plan for Faith to go to her Aunt Priscilla in Ticonderoga for the winter and attend school there.

"Oh! But that's New York. Why, the 'Yorkers' want to take all the Wilderness. I shouldn't want to go to school with 'Yorkers,'" Esther had responded, a little scornfully.

For she had often heard her father and his friends talk of the attempts made by the English officials of New York to drive the settlers on the New Hampshire Grants from their homes.

" 'Tis not the people of New York who would do us harm," Mrs. Carew had answered. "And Faith will make friends, I hope, with many of her schoolmates."

It was a beautiful October morning when Esther, seated in front of her father on the big gray horse, with the pumpkin-shell work-box wrapped in a safe bundle swinging from the front of the saddle, started for Brandon. Their way for most of the journey led over a rough trail. They would pass near the homes of many settlers, then over the lower slopes of Mooselamoo Mountain, and skirt Lake Dunmore, and would then find themselves on a smoother road for the remainder of their journey.

Faith walked beside the travelers to the edge of the wood and then the two little girls said good-bye.

"I'll come again in the spring," Esther called back.

Faith stood watching them until the branches of the trees hid them from sight. The maples seemed to be waving banners of scarlet leaves, and the slopes of the Green Mountains were beautiful in the glory of autumn foliage. The sun shone brightly, the sky was as blue as summer, and as Faith turned to run swiftly along the path to the mill she almost wished that she too was starting for a day's journey through the woods. The path ran along beside the mill-stream.

It seemed to Faith that the brook was traveling beside her like a gay companion, singing as it went. The little girl had had so few companions, none except an occasional visitor, that she had made friends with the birds and small woodland animals, and found companionship in the rippling music of the stream. There was a fine family of yellow-hammers just below the mill that Faith often visited, and she was sure that they knew her quite well. She had watched them build their nest in the early spring; had seen them bring food to the young birds, and had sat close by the nest while the young birds made their first efforts to fly. She knew where a fine silver-coated fox made its home on the rocky hillside beyond the garden-slope, and had told her father that "Silver-nose," as she had named the fox, knew that she was his friend, and would lie quite still at the entrance to its hole, while she would sit on a big rock not far distant.

But Faith was not thinking of these woodland friends as she ran along toward the mill; she was thinking of what she had heard her father say to Mr. Eldridge that morning. "Tell Colonel Allen the men of the Wilderness will be ready whenever he gives the word," Mr. Carew had said; and Mr. Eldridge had answered that it would not be long. Faith wondered what her father had meant, and if Colonel Allen would again visit the mill. She hoped he would, for he had seemed to know all about the woodland creatures, and had told Faith a wonderful story about the different months of the year. She thought of it now as she felt the warmth of the October sunshine.

"October is stirring the fire now," she called to her father, who was watching her from the door of the mill.

"What do you mean by that, child?" asked her father, smiling down at Faith's tanned face and bright eyes.

" 'Tis what Colonel Allen told me about the months. All twelve, every one of the year, sit about the fire. And now and then one of them stirs the fire, and that makes all the world warmer. July and August, when it is their turn, make it blaze; but the other months do not care so much about it. But once in a while each month takes its turn," answered Faith. "That's what Colonel Allen told me."

" 'Tis a good story," said Mr. Carew. "Did your mother tell you that I have sent word to your Aunt

Priscilla about your going to her house as soon as some trustworthy traveler going to Ticonderoga passes this way?"

"Yes, father. But I am learning a good deal at home. Mother says I read as well as she did when she was my age. And I can figure in fractions, and write neatly. I do not care much about school," answered Faith; for to be away from her mother and father all winter began to seem too great an undertaking.

"Yes, indeed; your mother tells me you learn quickly. But 'tis best for you to become acquainted with children of your own age. And you have never seen your cousins. Three boy cousins. Think of that. Why, your Aunt Prissy says that Donald is nearly as tall as you are; and he is but eight years old. And Hugh is six, and Philip four. Then there are neighbor children close at hand. You will play games, and have parties, and enjoy every day; besides going to school," responded her father encouragingly.

Then he told her of his own pleasant school days in the far-off Connecticut village where Grandmother Carew lived; and when Mrs. Carew called them to dinner Faith had begun to think that it would really be a fine thing to live with Aunt Priscilla and become acquainted with her little cousins, and all the pleasant, well-behaved children that her father described, with whom she would go to school and play games.

"It is nearly time for Kashaqua's yearly visit," said Mrs. Carew. "I have knit a scarf for her of crimson yarn. She generally comes before cold weather. Don't let her see your blue beads, Faith."

Faith did not make any answer. Kashaqua was an Indian woman who had appeared at the cabin every fall and spring ever since the Carews had settled there. When Faith was a tiny baby she had come, bringing a fine beaver skin as a gift for the little girl. She always came alone, and the family looked upon her as a friend, and always made a little feast for her, and sent her on her way laden with gifts. Not all the Indians of the Wilderness were friendly to settlers; and the Carews were glad to feel that Kashaqua was well disposed toward them. She often brought gifts of baskets, or of bright feathers or fine moccasins for Faith.

"I hope she will come before I go to Aunt Prissy's," said Faith. "I like Kashaqua."

"Kashaqua likes little girl."

Even Mr. Carew jumped at these words and the sudden appearance of the Indian woman standing just inside the kitchen door. She seemed pleased by their warm welcome, and sat down before the fire, while Faith hastened to bring her a good share of their simple dinner. Faith sat down on the floor beside her, greatly to Kashaqua's satisfaction, and told her about Esther Eldridge's visit, about the bear coming into the kitchen, and of how she had jumped from the window and run to the mill to tell her father. Kashaqua grunted her approval now and then.

"And what do you think, Kashaqua! I am to go to my Aunt Priscilla Scott, to Ticonderoga, and stay all winter," she concluded.

"Ticonderoga? When?" questioned Kashaqua, dipping a piece of corn bread in the dish of maple syrup.

"I am to go just as soon as some one goes over the trail who will take me," answered Faith.

"I take you. I go to Ticonderoga to-morrow. I take you," said Kashaqua.

CHAPTER VI

THE JOURNEY

"MOTHER dear, mother dear! Did you hear what Kashaqua says: that she will take me to Aunt Prissy's to-morrow?" said Faith.

The Indian woman had turned quickly, and her sharp little eyes were fixed on Mrs. Carew's face.

"You 'fraid let leettle girl go with Kashaqua?" she said, a little accusing note in her voice.

"No, indeed. Kashaqua would take good care of Faith. I know that. But to-morrow—" Mrs. Carew spoke bravely, but both Faith's father and mother were sadly troubled. To offend the Indian woman would mean to make enemies of the tribe to which she belonged; and then neither their lives nor their property would be safe; and she would never forgive them if they doubted her by refusing to let Faith make the journey to Ticonderoga in her care.

It was Faith who came to the rescue by declaring: "Oh, I'd rather go with Kashaqua than anybody. Mother dear, you said Aunt Prissy would see about my shoes and dresses. I don't have to wait to get ready," and Faith ran to her mother eager for her consent, thinking it would be a fine thing to go on a day's journey through the woods with the Indian woman, and quite forgetting for the moment that it meant a long absence from home.

Nothing could have pleased Kashaqua more than Faith's pleading. The half-angry expression faded from her face, and she nodded and smiled, grunting her satisfaction, and taking from one of her baskets a pair of fine doeskin moccasins, which she gave to Faith. "Present," she said briefly.

"They are the prettiest pair I ever had!" said Faith, looking admiringly at their fringed tops, and the pattern of a vine that ran from the toes to insteps, stitched in with thread-like crimson and blue thongs.

"It is a fine chance for Faith to go to her Aunt Priscilla," said Mr. Carew. "Do you know where Philip Scott lives, across Champlain?"

"Me know. Not great ways from Fort," responded Kashaqua. "Me take little girl safe to Scott's wigwam."

"That's right, Kashaqua," said Mr. Carew.

"Then me come back to mill and get meal an' get pie," said Kashaqua.

"Of course. I will make you the finest pie you ever tasted," said Mrs. Carew, with a little sigh of relief. For she had wondered how long it would be before they could get news that Kashaqua had kept her promise, and that Faith had reached her aunt's house in safety.

In the surprise and excitement of this new decision neither Faith nor her parents had much time to think about their separation. Although Aunt Priscilla was to see that Faith was well provided with suitable dresses, shoes, hat, and all that a little girl would need to wear to school and to church, there was, nevertheless, a good deal to do to prepare and put in order such things as she would take with her. Beside that Mrs. Carew meant to give the squaw a well-filled luncheon basket; so the remainder of the day went very quickly. Faith helped her mother, and talked gaily with Kashaqua of the good time they would have on the journey; while Kashaqua smoked and nodded, evidently quite satisfied and happy.

When night came the Indian woman made her preparations to sleep before the kitchen fire and the Carews went up-stairs to bed. The mother and father lay long awake that night. While they assured each other that Faith would be perfectly safe, and that the Indian woman would defend the little girl from all danger, they could not but feel an uncertainty. "We can trust the strength and love that has protected us always to go with our little maid," said Mr. Carew; "perhaps Kashaqua is the safest person we could find."

"We must hope so; but I shall not draw a good breath until she is here again, and tells me Faithie is safe with Priscilla," responded Mrs. Carew.

The little household was awake at an early hour the next morning. Faith was to wear the new moccasins. She wore her usual dress of brown homespun linen. Faith had never had a hat, or a pair of leather shoes, and only the simplest of linen and wool dresses. She had never before been away from home, except for a day's visit at the house of some neighboring settler. She knew that when she got to Aunt Prissy's she would have a hat, probably like the one Esther Eldridge had worn, ribbons to tie back her yellow curls, shining leather shoes, and many things that she had never before seen. She had thought a good deal about these things when planning for the journey, but now that the time was so near when she must say good-bye to her mother and father she forgot all about the good times in store, and wished with all her heart that she were not going.

"Don't let Kashaqua see you cry, child," her father whispered, seeing Faith's sad face; so she resolutely kept back her tears.

Breakfast was soon over. Kashaqua had stowed Faith's bundle of clothing in one of her baskets and swung it over her shoulder. The basket of luncheon also was secured by stout thongs and hung across her back, and they were ready to start.

"Be a good child, Faithie, dear," whispered Mrs. Carew.

"I'll fetch you home when it is April's turn to stir the fire," said her father smilingly, and Faith managed to smile back, and to say good-bye bravely, as she trudged down the path holding tight to Kashaqua's brown hand.

"I be back to-morrow night," Kashaqua called back, knowing that would be a word of comfort to the white woman who was letting her only child go from home.

Neither Faith nor Kashaqua spoke for some little time. At last Faith stopped suddenly and stood still, evidently listening. "I can't hear the brook," she said.

Kashaqua nodded, and the two walked on through the autumn woods. But now Kashaqua began to talk. She told Faith stories of the wild animals of the woods; of the traps she set along the streams to catch the martens and otters; and of a bear cub that the children of her village had tamed. But it had disappeared during the summer.

"The papooses catch birds and feed them," she continued, "tame birds so they know their name, and come right to wigwam." Faith listened eagerly, and began to think that an Indian village must be a very pleasant place to live.

"Where is your village, Kashaqua?" she asked.

"You not know my village? Way back 'cross Mooselamoo," answered Kashaqua.

"Perhaps I can go there some time," suggested Faith. But Kashaqua shook her head.

For several hours they walked steadily on through the autumn woods. They climbed several rocky ridges, crossed brooks, and carefully made their way over a swampy stretch of ground. Faith was very tired when Kashaqua finally swung the baskets and bundles from her shoulders and declared that it was time to eat.

The trail had led them up a hill, and as Faith, with a little tired sigh, seated herself on a moss-covered rock, she looked about with a little exclamation of wonder. Close beside the trail was a rough shelter made of the boughs of spruce and fir trees, and near at hand was piled a quantity of wood ready for a fire. There was a clearing, and the rough shelter was shaded by two fine oak trees.

"Does somebody live here?" asked Faith.

"Traveler's wigwam," explained Kashaqua, who was unpacking the lunch basket with many grunts of satisfaction. "White men going down the trail to big road to Shoreham sleep here," she added, holding up a fine round molasses cake in one hand and a roasted chicken in the other.

Faith was hungry as well as tired, and the two friends ate with good appetite. Kashaqua repacked the basket with what remained of the food, and with a pleasant nod to Faith declared she would "sleep a little," and curled herself up near the shelter.

Faith looked about the rough camp, and peered down the trail. She decided she too would sleep a little, and stretched herself out close beside Kashaqua, thinking that it was a wonderful thing to be so far from home,—nearly in sight of Lake Champlain, Kashaqua had told her, with an Indian woman for her guide and protector; and then her eyes closed and she was sound asleep.

It seemed to Faith that she had not slept a minute before she awakened suddenly, and found that Kashaqua had disappeared. But she heard a queer scrambling sound behind her and sat up and looked around. For a moment she was too frightened to speak, for a brown bear was clawing the remainder of their luncheon from the basket, grunting and sniffing, as if well pleased with what he found.

As Faith looked at him she was sure that this creature had dragged Kashaqua off into the woods, and that he might turn and seize her as soon as he had finished with the basket.

"Kashaqua! Kashaqua!" she called hopelessly. "What shall I do? What shall I do?"

There was a rustle of leaves close behind her and the Indian woman darted into the clearing. Without a word to Faith she ran straight to where the bear was crouched over the basket. Faith could hardly believe what she saw, for Kashaqua had seized the basket and pushed it out of the bear's reach, and was now belaboring him with a stout piece of wood that she had seized from the pile by the shelter. As she hit the bear she called out strange words in the Indian tongue, whose meaning Faith could not imagine, but which the bear seemed to understand. The creature accepted the blows with a queer little whimper which made Faith laugh in spite of her fear. And when Kashaqua had quite finished with him he crept along beside her, looking up as if pleading for forgiveness.

"Oh, Kashaqua! Is it the bear that your papooses tamed?" exclaimed Faith, remembering the story told her on the way.

Kashaqua nodded, at the same time muttering words of reproach to the bear.

"He like bad Indian, steal from friends," she explained to Faith. "His name Nooski," she added.

Nooski was quite ready to make friends with Faith, but she was not yet sure of his good-nature. It seemed to the little girl that the bear understood every word Kashaqua uttered; and when they went on their way down the trail Nooski followed, or kept close beside them.

It was still early in the afternoon when they reached level ground and Faith had her first glimpse of the blue waters of Lake Champlain and saw the heights of Ticonderoga on the opposite shore. For a moment she forgot Nooski and Kashaqua, and stood looking at the sparkling waters and listening to the same sound of "Chiming Waters" that had made the early French settlers call the place "Carillon." She wondered if she should ever see the inside of the fort of which she had heard so much, and then heard Kashaqua calling her name.

"Canoe all ready, Faith." The Indian woman had drawn the birch-bark canoe from its hiding-place in the underbrush, and the light craft now rested on the waters of the lake. The baskets and bundles were in the canoe, and Kashaqua, paddle in hand, stood waiting for her little companion.

"Where's Nooski?" asked Faith, looking about for the young bear.

Kashaqua pointed toward the distant range of mountains which they had left behind them. "He gone home," she said.

Kashaqua told her how to step into the canoe, and how to sit, and cautioned her not to move. Faith felt as if the day had been a wonderful dream. As Kashaqua with swift strokes of her paddle sent the canoe over the water Faith sat silent, with eyes fixed on the looming battlements of the fort, on the high mountain behind it, and thought to herself that no other little girl had ever taken such a journey.

Kashaqua landed some distance below the fort; the canoe was again safely hidden, and after a short walk across a field they reached a broad, well-traveled road. "'Most to Philip Scott's house," grunted Kashaqua. "You be glad?" and she looked down at the little girl with a friendly smile.

CHAPTER VII

NEW FRIENDS

"AN Indian woman and a little girl with yellow hair are coming across the road, mother," declared Donald Scott, rushing into the sitting-room, where his mother was busy with her sewing.

Mrs. Scott hastened to the front door. "Oh, Aunt Prissy," called Faith, running as fast as her tired feet could carry her, and hardly seeing the brown-haired little cousin standing by his mother's side.

Aunt Prissy welcomed her little niece, whom she had not expected to see for weeks to come, and then turned to thank Kashaqua. But the Indian woman had disappeared. The bundle containing Faith's clothing lay on the door-step, but there was no trace of her companion. Long afterward they discovered that Kashaqua had started directly back over the trail, and had reached the Carews' cabin, with her message of Faith's safe arrival at her aunt's house, early the next morning.

"Come in, dear child. You are indeed welcome. Your father's letter reached me but yesterday," said Aunt Prissy, putting her arm about Faith and leading her into the house. "I know you are tired, and you shall lie down on the settle for a little, and then have your supper and go straight to bed."

Faith was quite ready to agree. As she curled up on the broad sofa her three little cousins came into the room. They came on tiptoe, very quietly, Donald leading the two younger boys. Their mother had told them that Cousin Faith was tired after her long journey, and that they must just kiss her and run away.

Faith smiled up at the friendly little faces as they bent over to welcome her. "I know I shan't be lonesome with such dear cousins," she said, and the boys ran away to their play, quite sure that it was a fine thing to have a girl cousin come from the Wilderness to visit them.

Faith slept late the next morning, and awoke to hear the sound of rain against the windows. It was a lonesome sound to a little girl so far from her mother and father, and Faith was already thinking to herself that this big house, with its shining yellow floors, its white window curtains, and its nearness to a well-traveled road, was a very dreary place compared to her cabin home, when her chamber door opened and in came her Aunt Prissy, smiling and happy as if a rainy day was just what she had been hoping for.

"We shall have a fine time to-day, Faithie dear," she declared, as she filled the big blue wash-basin with warm water. "There is nothing like a rainy day for a real good time. Your Uncle Philip and the boys are waiting to eat breakfast with you, and I have a great deal to talk over with you; so make haste and come down," and Aunt Prissy, with a gay little nod, was gone, leaving Faith greatly cheered and wondering what the "good time" would be.

Uncle Philip Scott was waiting at the foot of the stairs. "So here is our little maid from the Wilderness! Well, it is a fine thing to have a girl in the house," he declared, leading Faith into the dining-room and giving her a seat at the table beside his own. "Did you have any adventures coming over the trail?" he asked, after Faith had greeted her little cousins.

Faith told them of "Nooski's" appearance, greatly to the delight of her boy cousins, who asked if the Indian woman had told Faith the best way to catch bear cubs and tame them.

"Come out to the shop, boys," said Mr. Scott as they finished breakfast, "and help me repair the cart, and fix 'Ginger's' harness. Perhaps Cousin Faith will come, too, later on in the morning."

"We'll see. Faithie and I have a good deal to do," responded Mrs. Scott.

The boys ran off with their father, chattering gaily, but at the door Donald turned and called back: "You'll come out to the shop, won't you, Cousin Faith?"

"If Aunt Prissy says I may," answered Faith.

"Yes; she will come," added Aunt Prissy, with her ready smile.

It seemed to Faith that Aunt Prissy was always smiling. "I don't believe she could be cross," thought the little girl.

She helped her aunt clear the table and wash the dishes, just as she had helped her mother at home; and as they went back and forth in the pleasant kitchen, with the dancing flames from the fireplace brightening the walls and making the tins shine like silver, Faith quite forgot that the rain was pouring down and that she was far from home.

"I am going to begin a dress for you this very day. It is some material I have in the house; a fine blue thibet, and I shall put ruffles on the skirt. That will be your Sunday dress," said Aunt Priscilla, "and your father wrote me you were to have the best shoes that the shoemaker can make for you. We'll see about the shoes to-morrow. Did you bring your blue beads, Faithie? But of course you did. They will be nice to wear with your blue frock. And I mean you to have a warm hood of quilted silk for Sunday wear."

Faith drew a long breath as her aunt finished. She wondered what Aunt Prissy would say if she told her about giving the blue beads to Esther Eldridge. But in the exciting prospect of so many new and beautiful things she almost forgot the lost beads. She had brought "Lady Amy," carefully packed in the stout bundle, and Aunt Prissy declared that the doll should have a dress and hood of the fine blue thibet.

"When shall I go to school, Aunt Prissy?" asked Faith.

"I think the school begins next week, and you shall be all ready. I mean to make you a good dress of gray and scarlet homespun for school wear," replied her aunt. "The schoolhouse is but a half-mile walk from here; a fine new cabin, and you and Donald may go together. I declare, the rain has stopped. 'Rain before seven, clear before eleven' is a true saying."

Faith ran to the window and looked out. "Yes, indeed. The sky is blue again," she said.

"You'd best run out to the shop a while now, Faithie. I'll call you when 'tis time," said her aunt.

Faith opened the kitchen door to step out, but closed it quickly, and looked around at her aunt with a startled face. "There's a little bear right on the door-step," she whispered.

"A bear! Oh, I forgot. You have not seen 'Scotchie,' our dog," said Aunt Prissy. "No wonder you thought he was a bear. But he is a fine fellow, and a good friend. I often wish your dear father had just such a dog," and she opened the door and called "Scotchie! Scotchie!"

The big black Newfoundland dog came slowly into the room.

"Put your hand on his head, Faith," said Aunt Prissy, "and I'll tell him who you are, and that he is to take care of you. He went to school with Donald all last spring, and we knew he would take care of him. Here, 'Scotchie,' go to the shop with Faith," she concluded.

Faith started for the square building on the further side of the yard, and the big dog marched along beside her. Donald and little Philip came running to meet her.

"I'm going to make you a bow and some arrows, Cousin Faith," said Donald, pushing open the shop door. "I have a fine piece of ash, just right for a bow, and some deerskin thongs to string it with. I made bows for Hugh and Philip."

The workshop seemed a very wonderful place to Faith, and she looked at the forge, with its glowing coals, over which her Uncle Philip was holding a bar of iron, at the long work-bench with its tools, and at the small bench, evidently made for the use of her little cousins.

The boys were eager to show her all their treasures. They had a box full of bright feathers, with which to tip their arrows.

"We'll show you how to make an arrow, Cousin Faith," said Donald. "First of all, you must be sure the piece of wood is straight, and has no knots," and Donald selected a narrow strip of wood and held it on a level with his eyes, squinting at its length, just as he had seen his father do. "This is a good straight piece. Here, you use my knife, and whittle it down until it's about as big as your finger. And then I'll show you how to finish it."

But before Faith had whittled the wood to the required size, they heard the sound of a gaily whistled tune, and Donald ran toward the door and called out: "Hallo, Nathan," and a tall, pleasant-faced boy of about fifteen years appeared in the doorway. He took off his coonskin cap as he entered.

"Good-morning, Mr. Scott," he said, and then turned smilingly to speak to the boys.

"Faith, this is Nathan Beaman," said Donald, and the tall boy bowed again, and Faith smiled and nodded.

"I've been up to the fort to sell a basket of eggs," explained Nathan, turning again to Mr. Scott.

"You are a great friend of the English soldiers, are you not, Nathan?" responded Mr. Scott.

"No, sir!" the boy answered quickly. "I go to the fort when my errands take me. But I know well enough what those English soldiers are there for; all the Shoreham folk know that. I wish the Green Mountain Boys held Ticonderoga," he concluded.

Mr. Scott rested a friendly hand on the boy's shoulder.

"Best not say that aloud, my boy; but I am glad the redcoats have not made you forget that American settlers have a right to defend their homes."

"I hear there's a reward offered for the capture of Ethan Allen," said the boy.

Mr. Scott laughed. "Yes, but he's in small danger. Colonel Allen may capture the fort instead of being taken a prisoner," he answered.

Nathan now turned toward the children, and Donald showed him the bow he was making for his cousin. "I'll string it for you," offered Nathan; and Donald was delighted to have the older boy finish his work, for he was quite sure that anything Nathan Beaman did was a little better than the work of any other boy.

"Who wants to capture Colonel Allen?" Faith asked.

"The 'Yorkers.' The English," responded the boy carelessly; "but it can't be done," he added. "Why, every man who holds a New Hampshire Grant would defend him. And Colonel Allen isn't afraid of the whole English army."

"I know him. He was at my father's house just a few weeks ago," said Faith.

"Don't tell anybody," said Nathan. "Some of the people at the fort may question you, but you mustn't let them know that you have ever seen Colonel Allen."

Donald had been busy sorting out feathers for the new arrows, and now showed Nathan a number of bright yellow tips, which the elder boy declared would be just what were needed.

Nathan asked Faith many questions about her father's mill, and about Ethan Allen's visit. And Faith told him of the big bear that had entered their kitchen and eaten the syrup. When Mrs. Scott called them to dinner she felt that she was well acquainted with the good-natured boy, whom Mrs. Scott welcomed warmly.

"I believe Nathan knows as much about Fort Ticonderoga as the men who built it," she said laughingly, "for the soldiers have let him play about there since he was a little boy."

"And Nathan made his own boat, too. The boat he comes over from Shoreham in," said Donald. For Nathan Beaman lived on the further side of the strip of water which separated Ticonderoga from the New Hampshire Grants.

That afternoon Faith and her aunt worked on the fine new blue dress. The next day Mrs. Scott took her little niece to the shoemaker, who measured her feet and promised to have the shoes ready at the end of a week.

As they started for the shoemaker's Mrs. Scott said:

"The man who will make your shoes is a great friend of the English soldiers. Your uncle thinks that he gathers up information about the American settlers and tells the English officers. Do not let him question you as to what your father thinks of American or English rule. For I must leave you there a little while to do an errand at the next house."

Faith began to think that it was rather a serious thing to live near an English fort.

CHAPTER VIII

THE SHOEMAKER'S DAUGHTER

THE shoemaker was the smallest man Faith had ever seen. She thought to herself that she was glad he was not an American. When he stood up to speak to Mrs. Scott Faith remembered a picture in one of her mother's books of an orang-outang. For the shoemaker's hair was coarse and black, and seemed to stand up all over his small head, and his face was nearly covered by a stubbly black beard. His arms were long, and he did not stand erect. His eyes were small and did not seem to see the person to whom he was speaking.

But he greeted his customers pleasantly, and as Faith sat on a little stool near his bench waiting for her aunt's return, he told her that he had a little daughter about her own age, but that she was not very well.

"Perhaps your aunt will let you come and see her some day?" he said.

"I'll ask her," replied Faith, and before they had time for any further conversation the door opened and a tall man in a scarlet coat, deerskin trousers and high boots entered the shop.

"Any news?" he asked sharply.

"No, captain. Nothing at all," replied the shoemaker.

"You're not worth your salt, Andy," declared the officer. "I'll wager this small maid here would have quicker ears for news."

Faith wished that she could run away, but did not dare to move.

"Well, another summer we'll put the old fort in order and have a garrison that will be worth while. Now, what about my riding boots?" he added, and after a little talk the officer departed.

It was not long before Mrs. Scott called for her little niece and the two started for home.

Faith told her aunt what the shoemaker had said about his little girl, and noticed that Aunt Prissy's face was rather grave and troubled.

"Do I have to go, Aunt Prissy?" she asked.

"We'll see, my dear. But now we must hurry home, and sew on the new dresses," replied Aunt Prissy, and for a few moments they walked on in silence.

Faith could hear the musical sound of the falls, and was reminded of the dancing mill-stream, of the silver fox and of her own dear "Bounce." Every hour since her arrival at Aunt Prissy's had been so filled

with new and strange happenings that the little girl
had not had time to be lonely.

"What is the name of the shoemaker's little girl,
Aunt Prissy?" she asked, as they came in sight of
home, with Donald and Philip, closely followed by
"Scotchie," coming to meet them.

"Her name is Louise Trent, and she is lame. She is
older than you, several years older," answered Aunt
Prissy, "and I fear she is a mischievous child. But the
poor girl has not had a mother to care for her for several years. She and her father live alone."

"Does she look like her father?" questioned Faith,
resolving that if such were the case she would not
want Louise for a playmate.

"Oh, no. Louise would be pretty if she were a neat
and well-behaved child. She has soft black hair,
black eyes, and is slenderly built. Too slender, I fear,
for health," replied Mrs. Scott, who often thought of
the shoemaker's motherless little girl, whose father
seemed to resent any effort to befriend her.

"Why, that sounds just the way Esther Eldridge
looks. Only Esther isn't lame," responded Faith;
and, in answer to her aunt's questions, Faith
described Esther's visit to the cabin, omitting,
however, the fact that she had given Esther the
blue beads.

Faith did not think to speak of the red-coated soldier until the family were gathered about the supper-table that night. Then she suddenly remembered what he had said, and repeated it to her uncle, who was asking her about her visit to Mr. Trent's shop.

"So that's their plan. More soldiers to come another summer! 'Twas a careless thing for an officer to repeat. But they are so sure that none of us dare lift a hand to protect ourselves that they care not who knows their plans. I'll see to it that Ethan Allen and the men at Bennington get word of this," said Mr. Scott, and then asked Faith to repeat again exactly what the officer had said.

In a few days both of Faith's new dresses were finished; and, greatly to her delight, Aunt Prissy had made her a pretty cap of blue velvet, with a partridge's wing on one side. She was trying on the cap before the mirror in the sitting-room one afternoon when she heard a queer noise on the porch and then in the front entry. Aunt Prissy was up-stairs, and the boys were playing outdoors.

"I wonder what it is?" thought Faith, running toward the door. As she opened it she nearly exclaimed in surprise, for there, leaning on a crutch, was the queerest little figure she had ever imagined. A little girl whose black hair straggled over her forehead, and whose big dark eyes had a half-frightened expression, stood staring in at the pleasant room. An old ragged shawl was pinned about her shoulders, and beneath it Faith could see the frayed worn skirt of gray homespun. But on her feet were a pair of fine leather shoes, well fitting and highly polished.

"I brought your shoes," said this untidy visitor, swinging herself a step forward nearer to Faith, and holding out a bundle. "Father doesn't know I've come," she added, with a little smile of satisfaction. "But I wanted to see you."

"Won't you sit down?" said Faith politely, pulling forward a big cushioned chair.

Louise Trent sat down as if hardly knowing if she dared trust the chair or not.

"Your aunt didn't let you come to see me, did she? I knew she wouldn't," continued Louise. "What you got?" she questioned, looking at the pretty cap with admiring eyes.

"It's new. And I never had one before," answered Faith.

"Well, I've never had one, and I never shall have. You wouldn't let me try that one on, would you?" said Louise, looking at Faith with such a longing expression in her dark eyes that Faith did not hesitate for a moment.

"Of course I will," she answered quickly, and taking off the cap placed it carefully on Louise's untidy black hair.

"If your hair was brushed back it would look nice on you," declared Faith. "You wait, and I'll get my brush and fix your hair," and before Louise could reply Faith was running up the stairs. She was back in a moment with brush and comb, and Louise submitted to having her hair put in order, and tied back with one of the new hair ribbons that Aunt Prissy had given Faith. While Faith was thus occupied Louise looked about the sitting-room, and asked questions.

"There," said Faith. "Now it looks nice on you. But what makes you wear that old shawl?"

Louise's face clouded, and she raised her crutch as if to strike Faith. "Don't you make fun of me. I have to wear it. I don't have nothing like other girls," she exclaimed, and dropping the crutch, she turned her face against the arm of the chair and began to sob bitterly.

For a moment Faith looked at her in amazement, and then she knelt down beside the big chair and began patting the shoulder under the ragged shawl.

"Don't cry, Louise. Don't cry. Listen, I'll ask my aunt to make you a cap just like mine. I know she will."

"No. She wouldn't want me to have a cap like yours," declared Louise.

"Isn't your father good to you?" questioned Faith. And this question made Louise sit up straight and wipe her eyes on the corner of the old shawl.

"Good to me! Of course he is. Didn't he make me these fine shoes?" she answered, pointing to her feet. "But how could he make me a pretty cap or a dress? And he doesn't want to ask anybody. But you needn't think he ain't good to me!" she concluded, reaching after the crutch.

"Don't go yet, Louise. See, that's my doll over on the sofa. Her name is 'Lady Amy,'" and Faith ran to the sofa and brought back her beloved doll and set it down in Louise's lap.

"I never touched a doll before," said Louise, almost in a whisper. "You're real good to let me hold her. Are you going to live here?"

"I'm going to school," replied Faith. "I've never been to school."

"Neither have I," said Louise. "I s'pose you know your letters, don't you?"

"Oh, yes. Of course I do. I can read and write, and do fractions," answered Faith.

"I can't read," declared Louise.

Just then Mrs. Scott entered the room. If she was surprised to see the shoemaker's daughter seated in her easy chair, wearing Faith's new cap and holding "Lady Amy," she did not let the little girls know it, but greeted Louise cordially, took Faith's new shoes from their wrapping and said they were indeed a fine pair of shoes. Then she turned to Louise, with the pleasant little smile that Faith so admired, and said: "You are the first little girl who has come to see my little niece, so I think it would be pleasant if you two girls had a taste of my fruit cake that I make just for company," and she started toward the dining-room and soon returned with a tray.

"Just bring the little table from the corner, Faithie, and set it in front of Louise and 'Lady Amy,'" she said, and Faith hastened to obey.

Aunt Prissy set the tray on the table. "I'll come back in a little while," she said, and left the girls to themselves.

The tray was very well filled. There was a plate of the rich dark cake, and beside it two dainty china plates and two fringed napkins. There was a plate of thin slices of bread and butter, a plate of cookies, and two glasses filled with creamy milk.

"Isn't this lovely?" exclaimed Faith, drawing a chair near the table. "It's just like a party, isn't it? I'm just as glad as I can be that you brought my shoes home, Louise. We'll be real friends now, shan't we?"

CHAPTER IX

LOUISE

"I MUST go home," said Louise, with a little sigh at having to end the most pleasant visit she ever remembered. The two little girls had finished the lunch, and had played happily with "Lady Amy." Mrs. Scott had left them quite by themselves, and not even the small cousins had come near the sitting-room.

As Louise spoke she took off the blue velvet cap, which she had worn all the afternoon, and began to untie the hair ribbon.

"Oh, Louise! Don't take off that hair ribbon. I gave it to you. It's a present," exclaimed Faith.

Louise shook her head. "Father won't let me keep it," she answered. "He wouldn't like it if he knew that I had eaten anything in this house. He is always telling me that if people offer to give me anything I must never, never take it."

Before Faith could speak Aunt Prissy came into the room.

"Tell your father I will come in and pay him for Faith's shoes to-morrow, Louise," she said pleasantly, "and you must come and see Faith again."

"Yes'm. Thank you," responded Louise shyly, and nodding to Faith with a look of smiling understanding, the crippled child made her way quickly from the room.

"Aunt Prissy, I like Louise Trent. I don't believe she is a mischievous girl. Just think, she never had a doll in her life! And her father won't let her take presents!" Faith had so much to say that she talked very rapidly.

"I see," responded her aunt, taking up the rumpled hair ribbon which Louise had refused. "I am glad you were so kind to the poor child," she added, smiling down at her little niece. "Tell me all you can about Louise. Perhaps there will be some way to make her life happier."

So Faith told her aunt that Louise could not read. That she had never before tasted fruit cake, and that she had no playmates, and had never had a present. "Why do you suppose she came to see me, Aunt Prissy?" she concluded.

"I cannot imagine. Unless it was because you are a stranger," replied Aunt Prissy. "I have an idea that I can arrange with Mr. Trent so that he will be willing for me to make Louise a dress, and get for her the things she ought to have. For the shoemaker is no poorer than most of his neighbors. How would you like to teach Louise to read?"

"I'd like to! Oh, Aunt Prissy, tell me your plan!" responded Faith eagerly.

"Wait until I am sure it is a good plan, Faithie dear," her aunt replied. "I'll go down and see Mr. Trent to-morrow. I blame myself that I have not tried to be of use to that child."

"May I go with you?" urged Faith.

"Why, yes. You can visit Louise while I talk with her father, since he asked you to come."

"Has the Witch gone?" called Donald, running into the room. "Didn't you know that all the children call the Trent girl a witch?" he asked his mother.

"No, Donald. But if they do they ought to be ashamed. She is a little girl without any mother to care for her. And now she is your cousin's friend, and we hope to see her here often. And you must always be polite and kind to her," replied Mrs. Scott.

Donald looked a little doubtful and puzzled.

"You ought to be more kind to her than to any other child, because she is lame," said Faith.

"All right. But what is a 'witch,' anyway?" responded Donald.

"It is a wicked word," answered his mother briefly. "See that you do not use it again."

Faith's thoughts were now so filled with Louise that she nearly lost her interest in the new dresses and shoes, and was eager for the next day to come so that she could again see her new friend.

Faith had been taught to sew neatly, and she wondered if she could not help make Louise a dress. "And perhaps Aunt Prissy will teach her how to make cake," she thought; for never to taste of cake seemed to Faith to be a real misfortune. For the first night since her arrival at her aunt's home Faith went to sleep without a homesick longing for the cabin in the Wilderness, and awoke the next morning thinking about all that could be done for the friendless little girl who could not accept a present.

"We will go to Mr. Trent's as soon as our morning work is finished," said Aunt Prissy, "and you shall wear your new shoes and cap. And I have a blue cape which I made for you before you came. The morning is chilly. You had best wear that."

"I don't look like Faith Carew, I am so fine," laughed the little girl, looking down at her shoes, and touching the soft cloth of the pretty blue cape.

As they walked along Faith told Aunt Prissy of her plans to teach Louise to sew, as well as to read. "And perhaps you'll show her how to make cake! Will you, Aunt Prissy?"

"Of course I will, if I can get the chance," replied her aunt.

The shoemaker greeted them pleasantly. Before Mrs. Scott could say anything of her errand he began to apologize for his daughter's visit.

"She slipped off without my knowing it. It shan't happen again," he said.

"But Faith will be very sorry if it doesn't happen again," replied Aunt Prissy. "Can she not run in and see Louise while I settle with you for the shoes?"

The shoemaker looked at her sharply for a moment, and then motioned Faith to follow him, leading the way across the shop toward a door on the further side of the room. The shop occupied the front room of the shoemaker's house. The two back rooms, with the chambers above, was where Louise and her father made their home.

Mr. Trent opened the door and said: "You'll find her in there," and Faith stepped into the queerest room that she had ever seen, and the door closed behind her. Louise was standing, half-hidden by a clumsy wooden chair. The shawl was still pinned about her shoulders.

"This ain't much like your aunt's house, is it? I guess you won't ever want to come again. And my father says I can't ever go to see you again. He says I don't look fit," said Louise.

But Faith's eyes had brightened, and she was looking at the further side of the room and smiling with delight. "Oh, Louise! Why didn't you tell me that you had a gray kitten? And it looks just like 'Bounce,'" and in a moment she had picked up the pretty kitten, and was sitting beside Louise on a roughly made wooden seat, telling her of her own kitten, while Louise eagerly described the cleverness of her own pet.

"What's its name?" asked Faith.

"Just 'kitten,'" answered Louise, as if surprised at the question.

"But it must have a real name," insisted Faith, and it was finally decided that it should be named "Jump," the nearest approach to the name of Faith's kitten that they could imagine.

The floor of the room was rough and uneven, and not very clean. There was a table, the big chair and the wooden seat. Although the morning was chilly there was no fire in the fireplace, although there was a pile of wood in one corner. There was but one window, which looked toward the lake.

"Come out in the kitchen, where it's warm," suggested Louise, after a few moments, and Faith was glad to follow her.

"Don't you want to try on my new cape?" asked Faith, as they reached the kitchen, a much pleasanter room than the one they had left.

Louise shook her head. "I daresn't," she replied. "Father may come in. And he'd take my head off."

"You are coming to see me, Louise. Aunt Prissy is talking to your father about it now," said Faith; but Louise was not to be convinced.

"He won't let me. You'll see," she answered mournfully. "*I* know. He'll think your aunt is 'Charity.' Why, he won't make shoes any more for the minister because his wife brought me a dress; and I didn't wear the dress, either."

But there was a surprise in store for Louise, for when Mrs. Scott and Mr. Trent entered the kitchen the shoemaker was smiling; and it seemed to Faith that he stood more erect, and did not look so much like the picture of the orang-outang.

"Louise, Mrs. Scott and I have been making a bargain," he said. "I am going to make shoes for her boys, and she is going to make dresses for my girl. Exchange work; I believe that's right, isn't it, ma'am?" and he turned to Mrs. Scott with a little bow.

"Yes, it is quite right. And I'll send you the bill for materials," said Aunt Prissy.

"Of course. Well, Louise, I warrant you're old enough to have proper dresses. And Mrs. Scott will take you home to stay with her until you are all fixed up as fine as this little maid," and the shoemaker nodded to Faith.

"Do you mean I'm to stay up there?" asked Louise, pointing in the direction of the Scotts' house. "I can't. Who'd take care of you, father?"

Mr. Trent seemed to stand very straight indeed as Louise spoke, and Faith was ashamed that she had ever thought he resembled the ugly picture in her mother's book.

"She's a good child," he said as if whispering to himself; but he easily convinced Louise that, for a few days, he could manage to take care of himself; and at last Louise, happy and excited over this change in her fortunes, hobbled off beside Mrs. Scott and Faith, while her father stood in the shop doorway looking after them.

It was a very differently dressed little daughter who returned to him at the end of the following week. She wore a neat brown wool dress, with a collar and cuffs of scarlet cloth, a cape of brown, and a cap of brown with a scarlet wing on one side. These, with her well-made, well-fitting shoes, made Louise a very trim little figure in spite of her lameness. Her hair, well brushed and neatly braided, was tied back with a scarlet ribbon. A bundle containing underwear, aprons, handkerchiefs, and hair ribbons of various colors, as well as a stout cotton dress for Louise to wear indoors, arrived at the shoemaker's house with the little girl.

Her father looked at her in amazement. "Why, Flibbertigibbet, you are a pretty girl," he declared, and was even more amazed at the gay laugh with which Louise answered him.

"I've learned a lot of things, father! I can make a cake, truly I can. And I'm learning to read. I'm so glad Faith Carew is going to live in Ticonderoga. Aren't you, father?"

Mr. Trent looked at his daughter again, and answered slowly: "Why, yes, Flibbertigibbet, I believe I am."

CHAPTER X

THE MAJOR'S DAUGHTERS

THE day that school began Faith returned home to find that a letter from her mother and father had arrived. It was a long letter, telling the little girl of all the happenings since her departure at the pleasant cabin in the Wilderness. Her father had shot a deer, which meant a good supply of fresh meat. Kashaqua had brought the good news of Faith's arrival at her aunt's house; and, best of all, her father wrote that before the heavy snows and severe winter cold began he should make the trip to Ticonderoga to be sure that his little daughter was well and happy.

But there was one sentence in her mother's letter that puzzled Faith. "Your father will bring your blue beads," her mother had written, and Faith could not understand it, for she was sure Esther had the beads. She had looked in the box in the sitting-room closet after Esther's departure, hoping that Esther might have put them back before starting for home, but the box had been empty.

"Who brought my letter, Uncle Phil?" she questioned, but her uncle did not seem to hear.

"Father got it from a man in a canoe when we were down at the shore. The man hid—,"

"Never mind, Hugh. You must not repeat what you see, even at home," said Mr. Scott.

So Faith asked no more questions. She knew that the Green Mountain Boys sent messengers through the Wilderness; and that Americans all through the Colonies were kept notified of what the English soldiers stationed in those northern posts were doing or planning. She was sure that some such messenger had brought her letter; and, while she wondered if it might have been her friend Ethan Allen, she had learned since her stay in her uncle's house that he did not like to be questioned in regard to his visitors from across the lake.

"I'll begin a letter to mother dear this very night, so it will be all ready when father comes," she said, thinking of all she longed to tell her mother about Louise, the school and her pretty new dresses.

"So you did not bring your beads," said Aunt Prissy, as she read Mrs. Carew's letter. "Did you forget them?"

Faith could feel her face flush as she replied: "No, Aunt Prissy." She wished that she could tell her aunt just why she had felt obliged to give them to Esther Eldridge, and how puzzled she was at her mother's reference to the beads. Faith was already discovering that a secret may be a very unpleasant possession.

As she thought of Esther, she recalled that her aunt had spoken of Louise as "mischievous," and Faith was quite sure that Louise would never have accepted the beads or have done any of the troublesome things that had made the first days of Esther's visit so difficult.

"Louise isn't mischievous," she declared suddenly. "What made you think she was, Aunt Prissy?"

Aunt Prissy was evidently surprised at this sudden change of subject, but she replied pleasantly:

"I ought not to have said such a thing; but Louise has improved every day since you became her friend. How does she get on in her learning to read?"

For Faith stopped at the shoemaker's house every day on her way home from school to teach Louise; and "Flibbertigibbet," as her father generally called her, was making good progress.

"She learns so quickly," replied Faith, "and she is learning to write. I do wish she would go to school, Aunt Prissy," for Louise had become almost sullen at the suggestion.

Faith did not know that Louise had appeared at the schoolhouse several years before, and had been so laughed at by some of the rough children of the village that she had turned on them violently and they had not dared come near her since. They had vented their spite, however, in calling, "Witch! Witch! Fly home on your broomstick," as Louise hobbled off toward home, vowing that never again would she go near a school, and sobbing herself to sleep that night.

Aunt Prissy had heard something of the unfortunate affair, and was glad that Louise, when next she appeared at school, would have some little knowledge to start with and a friend to help her.

"Perhaps she will go next term, now that she has a girl friend to go with her," responded Mrs. Scott.

Faith was making friends with two girls whose seats in the schoolroom were next her own. Their names were Caroline and Catherine Young. Faith was quite sure that they were two of the prettiest girls in the world, and wondered how it was possible for any one to make such beautiful dresses and such dainty white ruffled aprons as these two little girls wore to school. The sisters were very nearly of an age, and with their soft black curls and bright brown eyes, their flounced and embroidered dresses with dainty collars of lace, they looked very different from the more suitably dressed village children.

Caroline was eleven, and Catherine nine years old. But they were far in advance of the other children of the school.

They lost no time in telling Faith that their father was an English officer, stationed at Fort Ticonderoga; and this made Faith look at them with even more interest. Both the sisters were rather scornful in their manner toward the other school children. As Faith was a newcomer, and a stranger, they were more cordial to her.

"You must come to the fort with us some day," Caroline suggested, when the little girls had known each other for several weeks; and Faith accepted the invitation with such eagerness that the sisters looked at her approvingly. Their invitations to some of the other children had been rudely refused, and the whispered "Tories" had not failed to reach their ears.

"We like you," Caroline had continued in rather a condescending manner, "and we have told our mother about you. Could you go to the fort with us tomorrow? It's Saturday."

"Oh, yes; I'm sure I may. I have wanted to go to the fort ever since I came. You are real good to ask me," Faith had responded gratefully, to the evident satisfaction of the English girls who felt that this new little girl knew the proper way to receive an invitation.

It was settled that they would call for Faith early on Saturday afternoon.

"I may go, mayn't I, Aunt Prissy?" Faith asked, as she told her aunt of the invitation, and was rather puzzled to find that Aunt Prissy seemed a little doubtful as to the wisdom of permitting Faith visiting the fort with her new friends.

"It is a mile distant, and while that is not too long a walk, I do not like you to go so far from home with strangers," she said; but on Faith's declaring that the sisters were the best behaved girls in school, and that she had promised to go, Mrs. Scott gave her consent; and Faith was ready and waiting when Caroline and Catherine arrived, soon after dinner on Saturday.

"Is your father an officer?" asked Caroline, as the little girls started off.

Faith walked between her new friends, and looked from one to the other with admiring eyes.

"No, my father is a miller. And he owns a fine lot of land, too," she answered smilingly.

"Our father is a major. He will go back to Albany in the spring, and that is a much better place to live than this old frontier town," said Catherine. "We shan't have to play with common children there."

Faith did not quite know what Catherine meant, so she made no response, but began telling them of her own journey through the wilderness and across the lake. But her companions did not seem much interested.

"Your uncle is just a farmer, isn't he?" said Caroline.

"Yes, he is a farmer," Faith replied. She knew it was a fine thing to be a good farmer, so she answered smilingly. But before the fort was reached she began to feel that she did not like the sisters as well as when they set out together. They kept asking her questions. Did her mother have a silver service? and why did her aunt not have servants? As they neared the fort Catherine ran to her sister's side and whispered in her ear. After that they kept close together, walking a little way ahead of Faith. At the entrance to the fort Faith was somewhat alarmed to find a tall soldier, musket in hand. But he saluted the little girls, and Faith followed her companions along the narrow passageway. She wondered to herself what she had done to offend them, for they responded very stiffly to whatever she had to say. The narrow passage led into a large open square, surrounded by high walls. Faith looked about with wondering eyes. There were big cannons, stacks of musketry, and many strange things whose name or use she could not imagine. There were little groups of soldiers in red coats strolling about.

"Where is your father, Catherine?" she asked, and then looked about half fearfully; for both her companions had vanished.

None of the soldiers seemed to notice Faith. For a moment she looked about with anxious eyes, and then decided that her friends must have turned back to the entrance for some reason.

"And they probably think that I am right behind them," she thought, running toward an arched passageway which she believed was the one by which she had entered the fort. But it seemed much longer than when she came in a moment before. She began running, expecting to see the sisters at every step. Suddenly she found that she was facing a heavy door at the end of the passage, and realized that she had mistaken her way. But Faith was not frightened. "All I have to do is to run back," she thought, and turned to retrace her steps. But there were two passageways opening behind her at right angles. For an instant she hesitated, and then ran along the one to the right.

"I'm sure this is the way I came," she said aloud. But as she went on the passageway seemed to curve and twist, and to go on and on in an unfamiliar way. It grew more shadowy too. Faith found that she could not see very far ahead of her, and looking back it seemed even darker. She began to feel very tired.

"I'm sure Caroline and Catherine will come and find me," she thought, leaning against the damp wall of the passage. "I'll just rest a minute, and then I'll call so they will know which way to turn to find me."

CHAPTER XI

A DAY OF ADVENTURE

"Caroline! Caroline!" called Faith, and the call echoed back to her astonished ears from the shadowy passage. "I'd better go back! I'm sure the other was the right way," she finally decided; and very slowly she retraced her steps, stopping now and then to call the names of the girls who had deserted her.

It seemed a long time to Faith before she was back to where the big solid door had blocked the first passage. She was sure now that the other way would lead her back to the square where she had last seen her companions. But as she stood looking at the door she could see that it was not closed. It swung a little, and Faith wondered to herself if this door, after all, might not open near the entrance so that she could find her way to the road, and so back to Aunt Prissy.

She could just reach a big iron ring that swung from the center of the door; and she seized this and pulled with all her might. As the door slowly opened, letting in the clear October sunlight, Faith heard steps coming down the passage. The half-opened door nearly hid her from sight, and she looked back expecting to see either Caroline or Catherine, and, in the comfort of the hope of seeing them, quite ready to accept any excuse they might offer. But before she could call out she heard a voice, which was vaguely familiar, say: "I did leave that door open. Lucky I came back," and Nathan Beaman, the Shoreham boy, was close beside her.

When he saw a little girl still grasping the iron ring, he seemed too surprised to speak.

"I'm lost!" Faith whispered. "I'm so glad you came. Major Young's little girls asked me to come to the fort, and then ran away and left me," and Faith told of her endeavors to find her companions.

"Lucky I came back," said Nathan again, but this time his voice had an angry tone. "It was a mean trick. Those girls—" Then Nathan stopped suddenly. "Well, they're Tories," he concluded.

"I was afraid it was night," said Faith.

"No, but you might have wandered about in these passageways until you were tired out. Or you might have fallen from that door. Look out, but hold close to the door," said Nathan.

Faith came to the doorway and found herself looking straight down the face of a high cliff to the blue waters of the lake. Lifting her eyes she could look across and see the distant wooded hills of the Green Mountains, and could hear the "chiming waters" of the falls.

"It's lovely. But what do they have a door here for?" Faith asked.

And then Nathan explained what forts were for. That a door like that gave the soldiers who held the fort a chance to look up and down the lake in order to see the approach of an enemy by water. "And gives them a chance to scramble down the cliff and get away if the enemy captures the fort from the other side." Then he showed Faith the two big cannon that commanded the lake and any approach by the cliff.

"But come on. I must take you home," he declared, moving as if to close the door.

"Could we get out any other way than by going back through that passage?" asked Faith, who thought that she never wanted to see the two sisters again, and now feared they might be waiting for her.

"Certainly we could. That is, if you are a good climber," replied Nathan. "I'll tell you something, that is, if you'll never tell," he added.

"I won't," Faith declared earnestly.

"Well, I can go down that cliff and up, too, just as easily as I can walk along that passage. And the soldiers don't pay much attention to this part of the fort. There's a sentry at the other end of the passage, but he doesn't mind how I get in and out. If you'll do just as I say I'll take you down the cliff. My boat is hidden down by Willow Point, and I'll paddle you alongshore. 'Twill be easier than walking. That is, if you're not afraid," concluded Nathan.

"No, I'm not afraid," said Faith, thinking to herself that here was another secret, and almost wishing that she had not agreed to listen to it.

"Come on, then," said Nathan, stepping outside the door, and holding tightly to the door-frame with one hand and reaching the other toward Faith. "Hold tight to my hand and don't look down," he said. "Look to the right as you step out, and you'll see a chance for your feet. I've got a tight hold. You can't fall."

Faith clutched his hand and stepped out. There was room toward the right for her to stand. She heard the big door clang behind her. "I had to shut it," Nathan said, as he cautiously made his way a step down the face of the cliff. Faith followed cautiously. She noticed just how Nathan clung to the outstanding rocks, how slowly and carefully he made each movement. She knew if she slipped that she would push him as well as herself off into the lake.

"I mustn't slip! I mustn't," she said over and over to herself.

Nathan did not speak, except to tell her where to step. At last they were safely down, standing on a narrow rocky ledge which hardly gave them a foothold. Along this they crept to a thick growth of alder bushes where a clumsy wooden punt was fastened.

Faith followed Nathan into the punt, and as he pushed the boat off from the bushes she gave a long sigh of relief.

"That was great!" declared Nathan triumphantly. "Say, you're the bravest girl I know. I've always wondered if I could bring anybody down that cliff, and now I know I can. But you mustn't tell any one how we got out of the fort. You won't, will you?" And Faith renewed her promise not to tell.

Nathan paddled the boat out around the promontory on which the fort was built. He kept close to the shore.

"Does Major Young stay at the fort?" questioned Faith.

"Not very long at a time. He comes and goes, like all spies," replied Nathan scornfully. "I wish the Green Mountain Boys would take this fort and send the English back where they belong. They keep stirring the Indians up against the settlers, so that people don't know when they are safe."

It was the last day of October, and the morning had been bright and sunny. The sun still shone, but an east wind was ruffing the waters of the lake, and Faith began to feel chilly.

"I'll warrant you don't know when this lake was discovered?" said Nathan; and Faith was delighted to tell him that Samuel de Champlain discovered and gave the lake his name in 1609.

"The Indians used to call it 'Pe-ton-boque,'" she added.

But when Nathan asked when the fort was built she could not answer, and the boy told her of the brave Frenchmen who built Ticonderoga in 1756, bringing troops and supplies from Canada.

"The old fort has all sorts of provisions, and guns and powder that the English have stored there. I wish the American troops had them. If I were Ethan Allen or Seth Warner I'd make a try, anyway, for this fort and for Crown Point, too," said Nathan.

The rising wind made it rather difficult for the boy to manage his boat, and he finally landed some distance above the point where Kashaqua had reached shore. Faith was sure that she could go over the fields and find her way safely home, and Nathan was anxious to cross the lake to Shoreham before the wind became any stronger. Faith felt very grateful to him for bringing her from the fort.

"You'll be as brave as Colonel Allen when you grow up," she said, as she stood on the shore and watched him paddle off against the wind.

He nodded laughingly. "So will you. Remember your promise," he called back.

The wind seemed to blow the little girl before it as she hurried across the rough field. She held tight to her velvet cap, and, for the first time, wondered if she had torn or soiled the pretty new dress in her scramble down the cliff. Her mind was so full of the happenings of the afternoon that she did not look ahead to see where she was going, and suddenly her foot slipped and she fell headlong into a mass of thorn bushes, which seemed to seize her dress in a dozen places. By the time Faith had fought her way clear her hands were scratched and bleeding and her dress torn in ragged ugly tears that Faith was sure could never be mended.

She began to cry bitterly. "It's all the fault of those hateful girls," she sobbed aloud. "If they had not run off and left me I should be safe at home. What will Aunt Prissy say?"

Faith reached the road without further mishap, and was soon walking up the path. There was no one in sight; not even Scotchie was about. A sudden resolve entered her mind: She would slip up-stairs, change her dress, and not tell her aunt about the torn dress. "Perhaps I can mend it, after all," she thought.

As she changed her dress hurriedly, she wondered where all the family could be, for the house was very quiet. But she bathed her hands and face, smoothed her ruffled hair, and then looked for a place to hide the blue dress until she could find a chance to mend it. She peered into the closet. A small hair-covered trunk stood in the far corner and Faith lifted the top and thrust her dress in. At that moment she heard Donald's voice, and then her aunt's, and she started to go down-stairs to meet them.

CHAPTER XII

SECRETS

"Did you see all the fort, and the guns, and the soldiers?" asked Donald eagerly, running to meet his
cousin as she came slowly into the sitting-room.
"Why, your hand is all scratched!" he added in a surprised tone.

Faith tried to cover the scratched hand with a fold
of her skirt. Aunt Prissy noticed that the little girl
wore her every-day dress.

"Didn't you wear your blue dress, Faithie?" and
without waiting for an answer said: "Well, perhaps
this one was just as well, for you might have hurt
your blue dress."

Faith sat down on the big sofa thinking to herself
that she could never be happy again. First, and worst
of all, was the ruined dress. Then the remembrance
of the way she had been treated by Caroline and
Catherine; and, last of all, her *secrets!*—every one a
little more important and dreadful than the other.
First the blue beads; then Nathan's knowledge of a
hidden entrance to Fort Ticonderoga; and then the

dress. She was so taken up with her unhappy thoughts that she did not realize she had not answered Donald, or spoken to her aunt, until Donald, who was standing directly in front of her, demanded: "What's the matter, Cousin Faith? Does your tooth ache?"

Faith shook her head. "I'm tired. I didn't have a good time at all. I don't like those girls," and, greatly to Donald's alarm, she put her head on the arm of the sofa and began to cry.

In an instant she felt Aunt Prissy's arm about her, and heard the kind voice say: "Never mind, dear child. Don't think about them."

After a little Aunt Prissy persuaded Faith to lie down and rest until supper time.

"I'll sit here with my sewing and keep you company," said Aunt Prissy. "It's an hour to candle-light."

Donald tiptoed out of the room, but was back in a moment standing in the doorway and beckoning his mother; and Mrs. Scott went quietly toward him, closing the door softly behind her.

"It's those girls. The ones Faith went with to the fort," Donald explained in a whisper. "They're on the door-step."

Caroline and Catherine were standing, very neat and demure, at the front door.

"Has your little girl got home?" inquired Catherine in her most polite manner; "she ran off and left us," added Caroline.

"Faith is safe at home," responded Mrs. Scott in a pleasant voice.

"Why didn't you ask them to supper, mother? You said you were going to," demanded Donald, as he watched the sisters walk down the path.

"Your cousin is too tired for company," said his mother, who had planned a little festivity for Faith and her friends on their return, but had quickly decided that her little niece would be better pleased not to see the sisters again that day.

"All the more cake for us then," said Donald cheerfully, for he had seen a fine cake on the dining-room table; "there comes the shoemaker's girl," he added. "Shall you ask her to stay, mother?"

"Yes, indeed," and Mrs. Scott turned to give Louise a cordial welcome.

"Faith is resting on the sofa, but you may go right in, Louise. I know she will be glad to see you," she said, smiling down at the dark-eyed little girl. "When are you coming to make us another visit?"

"Father said I might stay all night if you asked me," responded Louise, who now felt sure that Mrs. Scott was her friend.

"We shall be glad indeed to have you, my dear. Let me take your cap and cape. And go in and cheer up Faithie, for I fear she has had an unhappy time," said Mrs. Scott.

Louise's smile faded. She had never had a friend until Faith Carew came to Ticonderoga, and the thought that any one had made Faith unhappy made her ready to inflict instant punishment on the offenders.

"Oh, Louise! I'm so glad it's you!" exclaimed Faith, as she heard the sound of Louise's crutch stubbing across the floor.

Louise sat down beside the crumpled little figure on the sofa.

"What did they do, Faith?" she demanded.

Faith told the story of the walk to the fort; of the disagreeable manner of both Caroline and Catherine toward her, and of their disappearance as soon as they were inside the fort. But she did not tell of her efforts to find them, nor of Nathan Beaman's appearance.

"They are hateful things!" Louise declared, "but it won't be long before they'll go to Albany with their father. "Oh!" she ended a little fearfully. "I ought not to have told that. It's a secret," she added quickly.

"No, it isn't. They told me," answered Faith, "and if it were a secret I shouldn't want to know it. I hate and despise secrets."

Louise looked at her friend with a little nod of comprehension. "That's because you have a secret," she said.

"How did you know, Louise?" and Faith wondered if it were possible Louise could know about the blue dress.

"I know," said Louise. "It's dreadful to know secrets. I can stay all night. My father has gone to the fort. Oh!" and again she put her hand over her mouth. "I ought not to have told that. He doesn't want any one to know."

Faith leaned back against the sofa with a little sigh of discouragement. It seemed to her there was nothing but secrets. She wished she was with her mother and father in her pleasant cabin home, where everybody knew about everything.

"Where's 'Lady Amy'?" asked Louise, quite sure that such a beautiful doll would comfort any trouble. And her question made Faith remember that Louise was a guest.

"I'll get her," she said, and in a few moments "Lady Amy" was sitting on the sofa between the two little friends, and Faith was displaying the new dresses that Aunt Prissy had helped her make for the doll.

"Father says he will buy me a doll," Louise announced, "and he's going to get me a fine string of

beads, too, when he goes away again;" for the shoemaker went away frequently on mysterious business.
Many of the settlers were quite sure that he carried
messages for the British officers to other forts; but
he came and went so stealthily that as yet no proof
was held against him.

"I have some blue beads. My father is going to
bring them when he comes to see me," said Faith. "I
hope yours will be just like them."

Louise shook her head a little doubtfully. "I may
never get them, after all. Father forgets things,"
she said.

Before supper time Faith was in a much happier
state of mind. She had helped Louise with her reading lesson; they had played that the sofa was a throne
and Lady Amy a queen, and that they were Lady
Amy's daughters; and the unpleasantness of the
early afternoon had quite vanished when the candles
were lighted, and supper on the table.

The supper seemed a feast to the shoemaker's
daughter. Every time she came to visit Faith Louise
tasted some new dish, so daintily prepared that she
was at once eager to learn to make it. Faith was hungry, too, and, as no reference was made to her trip to
the fort, she enjoyed her supper; and not until it was
finished was she reminded of her troubles.

"To-morrow Louise may go to church with us, and you may wear your blue dress that you are so careful of," Aunt Prissy said.

Faith made no response. She did not know what to do or say. She was so quiet that her aunt was sure her little niece was overtired, and soon after supper sent the little girls off to bed.

"What is the matter, Faith?" questioned Louise, when they were safely in the big chamber, with its high white bed, curtained windows, and comfortable chairs, and which to Louise seemed the finest bedroom in all the world.

Faith threw herself face down on the bed. "I don't know what to do! I don't know what to do! I've spoiled my blue dress!" she sobbed. There! That was one secret the less, she thought. And Louise would never tell. "I can't go to church. I don't dare tell Aunt Prissy about the dress. It was to be my best dress all winter," she added. "What shall I do, Louise?"

Louise shook her head. That Faith Carew, who seemed to her to be the most fortunate girl in all the world, should be in trouble was a far more dreadful thing to Louise than any trouble of her own.

"Let me see the dress," she said; "perhaps it isn't very bad."

Faith opened the trunk and pulled out the blue dress, which only that morning had been so fresh

and dainty. Now it was rumpled, soiled and torn.
Faith's tears flowed afresh as she held it out for
Louise to see.

"I guess you'd better tell your aunt," Louise said
soberly. "Tell her now, this minute," she added
quickly; "the sooner the better."

Faith looked at her in surprise. She wondered at
herself that she had hidden the dress, or even
thought of not telling Aunt Prissy.

"I'll go now," she said, and, still holding the dress,
walked out of the room. She no longer felt afraid. As
she went down the stairs she thought over all Aunt
Prissy's goodness toward her. "I'll tell her that I can
wear my other dress for best," she decided.

The boys were already in bed; Mr. Scott was
attending to the evening chores, and Aunt Prissy
was alone in the sitting-room when Faith appeared
in the doorway.

"Aunt Prissy, look! I tore my dress coming home to-
day, and I was afraid to tell you! Oh, Aunt Prissy!" for
her aunt had taken Faith and the blue dress into her
arms, and held the little girl closely as she said:

"Why, dear child! How could you ever be afraid of
me? About a dress, indeed! A torn dress is nothing.
Nothing at all."

"Louise, you are my very best friend," Faith
declared happily, as she came running into the

room a few minutes later. "I am so glad you made me tell."

Louise looked at Faith with shining eyes. She wished there was some wonderful thing that she could do for Faith as a return for all the happiness her friendship had brought into her life.

The clouds had lifted. Faith had disposed of one secret, and felt the others would not matter very much. The two little friends snuggled down in the big feather bed and were soon fast asleep.

CHAPTER XIII

LOUISE MAKES A PRESENT

THE week following Faith's visit to the fort proved rather a difficult one for her at school. Caroline and Catherine seemed to think they had played a fine joke, and accused her of running home when they were waiting for her. Faith had resolved not to quarrel with them, but apparently the sisters meant to force her into trouble, if sneering words and ridicule could do it.

"You're an American, so you don't dare talk back," sneered Catherine one day when Faith made no reply to the assertion that Faith had meant to run home from the fort alone.

"Americans are not afraid," replied Faith quickly.

Catherine jumped up and down with delight at having made Faith angry.

"Oh, yes they are. My father says so. Another summer the English soldiers are going to take all the farms, and all you rebels will be our servants," declared Catherine.

"Another summer the Green Mountain Boys will send the English soldiers where they will behave themselves," declared Faith. "Ethan Allen is braver than all the men in that fort."

"I don't care what you say. We're not going to play with you any more, are we, Caroline?" said Catherine. "You play with that horrid little lame girl."

"She isn't horrid. She is much better than you are. She wouldn't say or do the things you do!" responded Faith, now too angry to care what she said, "and she is my very best friend. I wouldn't play with you anyway. You're only Tory children," and Faith walked off with her head lifted very proudly, feeling she had won the battle; as indeed she had, for the sisters looked after her in silent horror.

To be called "only" Tory children was a new point of view, and for several days they let Faith wholly alone. Then one morning they appeared at school with the news that it would be their last appearance there.

"We're going to Albany, and never coming back to this rough common place," Catherine said.

"I am glad of it," Faith replied sharply; "perhaps you will learn to be polite in Albany."

Some of the other children overheard these remarks, and a little titter of amusement and satisfaction followed Faith's words. For the sisters had made no effort to be friendly with their schoolmates, and not one was sorry to see the last of them.

Faith awoke each morning hoping that her father would come that day, but it was toward the last of November before he appeared. There had been several light falls of snow; the ground was frozen and ice formed along the shores of the lake. The days were growing shorter, and Mrs. Scott had decided that it was best for Faith to come straight home from school at night, instead of stopping in to help Louise with her lessons. But both the little girls were pleased with the new plan that Mrs. Scott suggested, for Louise to come home with Faith on Tuesdays and Fridays and stay all night. Louise was learning a good deal more than to read and write. Mrs. Scott was teaching her to sew neatly, and Faith had taught her to knit. She was always warmly welcomed by Donald and the two younger boys, and these visits were the bright days of the week for Louise.

At last, when Faith had begun to think her father might not come after all, she returned from school one night to find him waiting for her. It was difficult to tell which of the two, father or daughter, was the happier in the joy of seeing each other. Mr. Carew had arrived in the early afternoon, and Aunt Prissy was now busy preparing the evening meal and Faith and her father had the sitting-room to themselves. There was so much to say that Faith hardly knew where to begin, after she had listened to all her father had to tell her of her mother.

"I would have come before, but I have been waiting for Kashaqua to come and stay with your mother," said Mr. Carew. "She appeared last night, and will stay until I return. And your mother could have no better protector. Kashaqua is proud enough since we proved our confidence in her by sending you here in her charge."

Faith told him about Louise, and was surprised to see her father's face grave and troubled. For Mr. Carew had heard of the shoemaker, and was sure that he was an English spy, and feared that his daughter's friendship with Faith might get the Scotts into some trouble.

"She is my dearest friend. I tell her everything," went on Faith.

"I'm afraid her father is not a friend to the settlers about here," replied Mr. Carew. "Be careful, dear child, that you do not mention any of the visitors who come to your uncle's house. Your friend would mean no harm, but if she told her father great harm might come of it," for Mr. Scott was doing his best to help the Americans. Messengers from Connecticut and Massachusetts with news for the settlers came to his house, and Mr. Scott found ways to forward their important communications to the men on the other side of Lake Champlain.

"Aunt Prissy likes Louise; we all do," pleaded Faith; so her father said no more, thinking that perhaps he had been over-anxious.

"Your mother sent your blue beads. I expect you would have been scolded a little for being a careless child if you had been at home, for she found them under the settle cushion the very day you left home," said Mr. Carew, handing Faith two small packages. "The larger package is one that came from Esther Eldridge a few weeks ago," he added, in answer to Faith's questioning look.

"I wonder what it can be," said Faith; but before she opened Esther's package she had taken the blue beads from the pretty box and put them around her neck, touching them with loving fingers, and looking down at them with delight. Then she unfastened the wrapping of the second package.

"Here is a letter!" she exclaimed, and began reading it. As she read her face brightened, and at last she laughed with delight. "Oh, father! Read it! Esther says to let you and mother read it. And she has sent me another string of beads!" And now Faith opened the other box, a very pretty little box of shining yellow wood with "Faith" cut on the top, and took out another string of blue beads, so nearly like her own that it was difficult to tell them apart.

Mr. Carew read Esther's letter. She wrote that she had lost Faith's beads, and had been afraid to tell her. "Now I am sending you another string that my father got on purpose. I think you were fine not to say a word to any one about how horrid I was to ask for your beads. Please let your mother and father read this letter, so they will know how polite you were to company."

"So it was Esther who lost the beads! Well, now what are you going to do with two strings of beads?" said her father smilingly.

When Aunt Prissy came into the room Faith ran to show her Esther's present and the letter, and told her of what had happened when she had so rashly promised to give Esther anything she might ask for. "I am so glad to have my own beads back again. And most of all I am glad not to have the secret," she said, thinking to herself that life was much happier when father and mother and Aunt Prissy could know everything that she knew. Then, suddenly, Faith recalled the fort, and the difficult climb down the cliff. "But that's not my secret. It's something outside. Something that I ought not to tell," she thought, with a little sense of satisfaction.

"But which string of beads did Esther send you? I can't tell them apart," she heard Aunt Prissy say laughingly.

When the time came for Mr. Carew to start for home Faith was sure that she wanted to go home with him. And it was only when her father had promised to come after her early in March, "or as soon as March stirs the fire, and gives a good warm day," he said, that Faith could be reconciled and persuaded to let him go without her. She was glad indeed that it was a Tuesday, and that Louise would come to stay all night. Faith was eager to tell Louise the story of the blue beads, and to show her those Esther had sent, and those that Aunt Prissy had given her. Faith was sure that she herself could tell the beads apart, and equally sure that no one else could do so.

Louise was waiting at the gate when Faith came from school. At the first sight of her Faith was hardly sure that it was Louise; for the little girl at the gate had on a beautiful fur coat. It was made of otter skins, brown and soft. On her head was a cap of the same fur; and, as Faith came close, she saw that Louise wore fur mittens.

"Oh, Louise! Your coat is splendid," she exclaimed. "And you look so pretty in it; and the cap and mittens." And Faith looked at Louise, smiling with delighted admiration.

Louise nodded happily. "My father sent to Albany for them. A man brought them last night," she said. "You do truly like them?" she questioned, a little anxiously.

"Of course! Any girl would think they were beautiful. Aunt Prissy will be just as glad as I am," declared Faith. "What's in that big bundle?" she added, as Louise lifted a big bundle from beside the gate.

But if Louise heard she made no reply, and when Faith offered to carry the package she shook her head laughingly. Faith thought it might be something that Louise wanted to work on that evening, and was so intent on telling of her father's visit, the blue beads, and the promised visit to her own dear home in March, that she did not really give much thought to the package.

Aunt Prissy was at the window watching for the girls, with the three little boys about her. They all came to the door, and Aunt Prissy exclaimed, just as Faith had done, over the beauty of Louise's new possessions. "But what is in that big bundle, Louise?" she asked, when the little lame girl had taken off coat, cap and mittens and stood smiling up at her good friend.

"Once you said to me that a present was something that any one ought to be very happy to receive," she said.

"Yes, I remember. And I know you are happy over your father's gift," replied Mrs. Scott.

Louise nodded, and began unwrapping the bundle.

"This is my present to Faith," she said, struggling to untie the heavy string.

"Let me, Louise; let me," and Donald was down on his knees and in a moment the bundle was opened, and Donald exclaimed:

"My! It's a coat exactly like Louise's."

"There's a cap too, and mittens," said Louise eagerly. "Do try it on."

Donald stood holding the coat; and Faith, as excited and happy as Louise, slipped on the coat, put the cap on her head and held out her hands for the mittens.

"Oh, Louise! They are lovely. I may keep them, mayn't I, Aunt Prissy?" she asked, turning about for her aunt to see how nicely the coat fitted.

Neither of the little girls noticed that Mrs. Scott looked grave and a little troubled, for she was thinking that this was almost too fine a present for her little niece to accept from the shoemaker's daughter. But she knew that to refuse to let Faith accept it would not only make both the girls very unhappy, but that Mr. Trent would forbid Louise coming to the house, and so stop all her friendly efforts to help Louise; so she added her thanks to those of Faith, and the two little friends were as happy as it is possible to be over giving and receiving a beautiful gift. Faith even forgot her blue beads in the pleasure of possessing the pretty coat and cap.

CHAPTER XIV

A BIRTHDAY

"CAN you skate, Cousin Faith?" asked Donald, on their way to school one morning in late December. There had been a week of very cold weather, and the ice of the lake glittered temptingly in the morning sun.

"No, I never had any skates, and there wasn't a very good chance for skating at home," answered Faith regretfully; for many of the school children were eager for the sport, and told her of their good times on the ice.

"Mother has a pair of skates for you; I heard her say so; and father is going to teach you to skate," responded Donald. "I can skate," he added, "and after you learn we'll have a fine time. Nat Beaman comes across the lake on the ice in no time."

It was rather difficult for Faith to pay attention to her studies that day. She wondered when Aunt Prissy would give her the skates, and Uncle Phil teach her how to use them. And when the schoolmaster announced that there would be no school for the remainder of the week Faith felt that everything was planned just right for her. Now, she thought, she could begin the very next day, if only the cold, clear weather would continue.

The sun set clear and red that night, and the stars shone brightly. Faith was sure the next day would be pleasant. Donald found a chance to tell Faith that the skates were a "secret." "But I didn't know it until just a few minutes ago," he explained, adding briefly: "I hate secrets."

Faith agreed heartily. If the skates were a secret who could tell when Aunt Prissy would give them to her? She went to bed a little despondent, thinking to herself that as soon as she was clear of one secret another seemed ready to interfere with her happiness. But she was soon asleep, and woke up to find the sun shining in at her windows, and Aunt Prissy starting the fire with a shovelful of coals from the kitchen hearth. And what were those shining silver-like objects swinging from the bed-post?

"Skates! My skates!" she exclaimed, sitting up in bed. "Oh, Aunt Prissy! I did want them so to-day."

"They are your birthday present from your father and mother," said Aunt Prissy, coming to the side of the bed, and leaning over to kiss her little niece. "Eleven years old to-day! And you had forgotten all about it!"

"Why, so I am! Why, so I did!" said Faith. "Well, I like secrets that end this way. May I go skating right away, Aunt Prissy?"

"Breakfast first!" laughed Aunt Prissy, and was out of the room before Faith had noticed that lying across the foot of her bed was a dress of pretty plaided blue and brown wool. A slip of paper was pinned to it: "For Faith to wear skating," she read.

"Lovely! Lovely!" exclaimed Faith, as she hastened to dress in front of the blazing fire.

"Why, here are new stockings, too," she said, as she discovered a pair of warm knit brown and blue stockings.

She came running into the dining-room, skates in hand, to be met by her uncle and little cousins with birthday greetings. Donald had at last finished the bow and arrows that he had promised her weeks before, and now gave them to her; Hugh had made a "quiver," a little case to hold the arrows, such as the Indians use, of birch bark, and little Philip had a dish filled with molasses candy, which he had helped to make.

It was a beautiful morning for Faith, and the broiled chicken and hot corn cake gave the breakfast an added sense of festivity.

Soon after breakfast Mr. Scott, Donald and Faith were ready to start for the lake. Donald took his sled along. "So we can draw Cousin Faith home, if she gets tired," he explained, with quite an air of being older and stronger than his cousin.

Aunt Prissy watched them start off, thinking to herself that Faith had never looked so pretty as she did in the fur coat and cap, with her skates swinging from her arm, the bright steel catching the rays of sunlight.

They crossed the road, and went down the field to the shore. The hard crust gave Faith and Donald a fine coast down the slope, and both the children exclaimed with delight when Mr. Scott, running and sliding, reached the shore almost as soon as they did.

Mr. Scott fastened on Faith's skates, and held up by her uncle on one side and Donald on the other, Faith ventured out on the dark, shining ice. After a few lurches and tumbles, she found that she could stand alone, and in a short time could skate a little.

"Father, are those Indians?" asked Donald, pointing to a number of dark figures coming swiftly down the lake from the direction of the fort.

Mr. Scott looked, and answered quickly: "Yes. They have seen us; so we will skate toward them. They will probably be friendly." But he told Faith to sit down on the sled, and took fast hold of Donald's hand. In a few moments the flying figures of the Indians were close at hand. There were six of them, young braves, and evidently racing either for sport, or bound on some errand of importance, for they sped straight past the little group, with a friendly call of salutation.

"I wonder what that means," said Mr. Scott, turning to watch them. "It may be they are on their way to Albany as messengers from the fort," he added, as if speaking to himself.

"What kind of a message, Uncle Philip?" asked Faith.

"Heaven knows, child. Perhaps for troops enough to crush the American settlers, and drive them from their homes," replied Mr. Scott. For news of the trouble in Boston, the blockade of the port, and the lack of supplies, had reached the men of the Wilderness; and Mr. Scott knew that the English were planning to send a larger body of troops to Fort Ticonderoga and Crown Point, and the sight of these speeding Indians made him wonder if they might not be English messengers.

"Couldn't we stop them, uncle?" asked Faith, so earnestly that her uncle looked down at her in smiling surprise.

"Couldn't we? It will be dreadful to leave our homes," said Faith.

Mr. Scott swung the little girl gently around. "Look!" he said, pointing down the lake. Already the

Indians were but dark specks in the distance. "If trouble comes there are brave Americans ready," he said; "and now we had best be going toward home, or you will be too tired to come out this afternoon."

Faith and Donald were surprised to find that it was dinner time. They had a great deal to tell Aunt Prissy of their morning's adventures.

"Could a little girl do anything to help, Aunt Prissy, if the English do try to drive us away?" Faith asked, as she helped her aunt clear the dining-room table.

"Who knows?" responded Mrs. Scott, cheerfully. "A brave girl might be of great service. But I do not believe the Tories will dare go much farther. At all events, we will be ready for them. Run to the door, Faithie; there comes Louise."

Louise was as pleased over Faith's presents as Faith herself, and delighted at the prospect of going to the lake with Faith and Donald that afternoon. Faith and Donald promised to draw her on the sled, and Aunt Prissy was to be their companion.

"Mother can skate like a bird," Donald declared admiringly.

Louise was no longer the sullen, sad-faced child whom Faith had first seen. She knew that she had friends; she was included in all the pleasant happenings with Faith; her father seemed to take pride in her appearance; and best of all, she thought, she was to begin school when the spring term opened. To-day as they started off for the lake she was as full of happiness as any child could be.

There were a number of children and young people on the ice, skating and sliding. A number of boys had built a bonfire on the shore, where they could warm their chilled toes and fingers.

Nathan Beaman was there, circling about in skilful curves, or darting off with long swift strokes, greatly to the admiration of the other children. He was quite ready to take the sled rope and give Louise a fine ride up the lake toward the fort, and back to the fire, and to guide Faith in her clumsy efforts to skate.

Faith and Louise were warming their fingers at the fire when they heard loud voices and a commotion on the ice.

"What is it? Indians?" exclaimed Faith, looking around, for the settlers never knew at what moment the Indians might become mischievous.

"No! Soldiers. Soldiers from the fort," replied Aunt Prissy, drawing the little girls away from the fire. "Perhaps they are only coming to warm their fingers."

Two red-coated soldiers came swinging close to the shore. They were talking loudly, and as they neared the fire they called out: "Clear away from that fire. We'll have no fires built on this shore. 'Tis too good a way to send messages across the lake."

With a couple of stout sticks they beat out the flame, kicking snow over the coals, and extinguishing the last bit of fire.

Mrs. Scott had helped Louise toward the ice, but Faith had lingered a moment. As one of the soldiers turned from the fire he found himself facing a little fur-clad figure with flushed cheeks and angry eyes.

"That was our fire. You had no business to put it out," Faith declared.

"Oh, ho! What's this?" laughed the soldier. "Do you own this lake? Or perhaps you are our new captain?"

"It is a mean thing to spoil our fire," continued Faith; "we wouldn't do you any harm."

"I'm not so sure about that," replied the soldier. "You have a pretty fierce expression," and with another kick at the fire, and a "good-bye, little rebel," to Faith, the two soldiers started back to the fort. The skaters now, troubled and angry by the unfriendly interference, were taking off their skates and starting for home.

"I wish American soldiers were in that fort," said Nat Beaman.

"Why don't you ask Colonel Allen to come and take it?" asked Faith earnestly; she was quite sure that Ethan Allen could do anything he attempted.

"Ask him yourself," responded Nathan laughingly.

"I guess I will," Faith thought to herself, as she followed Aunt Prissy up the field toward home. "Perhaps that would be doing something to help Americans."

The more Faith thought about this the stronger became her resolve to ask Colonel Allen to take possession of Fort Ticonderoga. She was so silent all the way home that her companions were sure she was overtired. Louise had to return to her own home, and soon after supper Faith was ready to go to bed.

"I've got a real secret now; even if I don't like secrets," she thought to herself. For she realized that she could not tell any one of her determination to find some way to ask Ethan Allen to capture Ticonderoga and send the troublesome English soldiers back to their own homes.

CHAPTER XV

NEW ADVENTURES

"It will be a good day to put a quilt in the frame," said Aunt Prissy, the morning after Faith's birthday. "You and Donald can help me with it right after breakfast; then while you children are off to the lake I will mark the pattern."

"Can't I help mark the pattern?" asked Faith, who had sometimes helped her mother, and thought it the most interesting part of the quilting.

The quilting-frame, four long strips of wood, was brought into the sitting-room and rested on the backs of four stout wooden chairs, forming a square. The frame was held firmly together at the corners by clamps and screws, so that it could be changed and adjusted to fit the quilt.

This quilt was a very pretty one, Faith thought, as she watched Aunt Prissy fasten it to the frame with stout linen thread. It was made of bits of bright woolen cloth. There were pieces of Faith's new dresses, and of the dresses made for Louise, and they were neatly stitched together in a diamond-shaped pattern. Faith had made a good many of these, and so

132

had Louise in the evenings as they sat with Aunt Prissy before the open fire.

First of all Aunt Prissy had fastened the lining for the quilt to the frame. Over this she spread an even layer of soft wool, and then over this the bright patchwork was spread and fastened. And now it was ready to mark the quilting pattern.

Aunt Prissy took a ball of firm twine and rubbed it well with white chalk. The cord was fastened tightly across the surface of the quilt.

"Now," said Aunt Prissy, and Faith took the tight cord up and "snap" it went when her fingers released their hold, leaving a straight white mark across the quilt. Back and forth they stretched the cord and "snapped" the line, until the quilt was marked in a checkerboard pattern of white lines, which the quilters would follow with their neat stitches.

"I believe I'll have a quilting bee to-morrow," said Aunt Prissy. "When you and Donald start out you can go down and ask the minister's wife, and be sure and say that we shall expect Mr. Fairbanks to tea. Then ask Neighbor Willis and her husband, and Mrs. Tuttle. I think that will be a pleasant number."

"May I help quilt?" asked Faith.

"Of course you may. Tell Mrs. Tuttle to bring her daughter. And now, my dear, in what manner will you ask our friends to the quilting party and to tea?"

asked Aunt Prissy, looking down at her little niece with her pretty smile.

"I shall rap at the minister's door first, of course; and when Mrs. Fairbanks opens the door I shall make my best curtsy, like this:" and Faith took a bit of her skirt in each hand, and bent in a very pretty curtsy indeed; "and I shall say: 'Good-morning, Mrs. Fairbanks. My Aunt Prissy will be very happy if you and the minister will come to her quilting bee tomorrow afternoon and stay to tea.'"

Aunt Prissy nodded approvingly. "I think that will do very nicely indeed. Now put on your things and run along. Donald is waiting."

Donald and "Scotchie" were at the door when Faith was ready to start. The big dog barked his delight at being allowed to go with the children.

"I'd like to harness him to the sled; he could draw us both," suggested Donald, but Faith was sure that "Scotchie" would upset the sled; so her cousin gave up the project.

"We can go on the lake just below Mrs. Tuttle's house, and skate along the shore home; can't we, Cousin Faith?" asked Donald, after they had stopped at Mrs. Willis' house and that of the clergyman.

"Let's call and get Louise," suggested Faith.

"Oh, there won't be time. Look, there goes an English soldier into the shoemaker's now. The boys all say that the shoemaker is an English spy," answered Donald.

They were nearly in front of Mr. Trent's shop now, and Faith noticed that the soldier was the one who had been on the lake the previous day, and who had called her "a little rebel."

"Come to the back door, Donald. Just a moment, while I speak to Louise. And make 'Scotchie' keep still," said Faith, turning into the path leading to the back door.

"Scotchie" was barking fiercely as if he resented the sight of the redcoat.

The soldier tuned quickly. "Stop that dog before I put a bullet into him," he called.

"He's afraid," Donald whispered to Faith, with a word to "Scotchie," and Faith ran up the path and entered the house.

Donald and "Scotchie" stood waiting, the dog growling now and then, whenever the soldier moved about on the door-step. It was evident that the shoemaker was not at home, for no answer came to the raps. In a moment Louise appeared at the door and told the man that her father was not at home.

"Send that boy with the dog about his business," said the soldier.

"'Tis the public road, sir; and 'tis not likely he'd mind what I might say," responded Louise smilingly, as she closed the door.

Donald rested his mittened hand on "Scotchie's" head.

"You needn't be afraid. I won't let him hurt you," Donald called.

The soldier came down the path scowling.

"I've a great mind to kick the beast," he said.

"You'd better not," said Donald.

Evidently the man agreed, for he went past as quickly as possible. Donald watched him with a little scornful smile. The boy was not old enough to realize, as Faith did, the difference between these hired soldiers of England, and the brave Americans who were ready to undertake any sacrifice to secure the freedom of their country, but he was a brave boy, and thought poorly of this soldier's courage.

Louise listened to Faith's hurried account of the proposed quilting party.

"And you must come too, Louise," she concluded, "and come early."

Louise promised. She had never been to a quilting party, and was sure that it would be a great experience. She could not go to the lake, for she must not leave the house until her father returned.

When Faith rejoined Donald he told her of the soldier's evident fear of the dog. "I don't see what made 'Scotchie' growl so," added Donald.

"I'm glad he did," responded Faith. "Come on; let's hurry, or we won't have much time on the ice," so off they went across the field.

But as they reached the shore they looked at each other questioningly. The lake seemed to be in the possession of the redcoats. At least half the garrison of the fort were on the ice; skating, racing, and evidently enjoying themselves.

"We had better go home," said Faith, and Donald made no objections. The two children, disappointed of their morning's sport, went slowly back toward home.

"That's the way they take everything," declared Faith, renewing her promise to herself to try in some way to let Ethan Allen know how easy it would be to drive the English from Ticonderoga.

"I am glad you did not venture on the ice," Aunt Prissy said when Donald and Faith told their story. "The English become less friendly every day. Well, we will not think of them when there is so much to do as we have before us."

"I asked Louise to come to the quilting," said Faith.

"That's right; and I am going to send Donald to ask a number of your schoolmates to come in the evening.

The moon will be full to light them home, and you children can have the kitchen to yourselves after supper, and make molasses candy," said Aunt Prissy.

This seemed a very delightful idea to both Faith and Donald. The thought of making candy reminded Faith of Esther Eldridge, and of the bear's sudden appearance at the kitchen door. Mr. Carew had promised Faith to ask Esther's father to bring her to visit Faith on her return home, and Faith often thought of how much she and Esther would have to tell each other.

That afternoon Faith helped her Aunt Prissy in preparing for the quilting. Aunt Prissy was cooking a ham, and the brick oven held some of the spiced cakes that the children liked so well. Donald cracked a big dish full of hickory-nuts, while Faith rubbed the pewter plates and pitchers until they shone like silver. The two younger boys ran in and out of the kitchen, thinking a quilting party must be a great affair.

Mr. Scott had been cutting wood at the edge of the forest, and did not return until nearly dusk; and when he arrived there was a man with him—evidently a traveler, for there was a pack on his back, and he was tired. Faith heard her Aunt Prissy call the stranger by name, and welcome him.

"Why, it is Esther's father. Of course it is!" she exclaimed suddenly.

Mr. Eldridge told her all about Esther, and promised that his little daughter should again visit the Wilderness cabin. Faith wondered what business it was that took Mr. Eldridge through the Wilderness and up and down the lakes. Long afterward she discovered that he was one of the trusted messengers of the American leaders, and through him the American settlers along the lake shores and through the New Hampshire Grants were kept informed of what the English were doing. She did not know that he underwent constant danger.

The little boys went early to bed that night, but Faith was not sleepy. The firelight in the sitting-room made dancing pictures on the wall, as she sat in a small chair at the end of the sofa. The sound of Aunt Prissy's knitting needles made her think of the silvery tinkle of the mill-stream under the winter ice in her Wilderness home. Mr. Eldridge and her uncle were talking quietly. She heard her uncle say that: "Ticonderoga was the lock to the gate of the country," and Mr. Eldridge respond that until Crown Point and Ticonderoga were taken by the Americans that none of the colonies could be safe.

"If there were any way to get into Fort Ticonderoga," said Mr. Eldridge. "They say there's a secret passageway."

Faith was all attention at this. She quite forgot that she was listening to conversation not intended for her ears, as she heard her uncle answer:

"There is such a door, but no way for an American to find it. If some one could get entrance to the fort in that way, discover just the plan of the place, and escape, it would be of the greatest service to the Americans when the right time came to take the fort."

"Time for bed, Faithie," said Aunt Prissy, and, very reluctantly, the little girl went up stairs. She was thinking of all that her uncle and Mr. Eldridge had said, and of the unguarded door opening on the cliff at the fort. She wondered if she could make her way up that steep cliff as easily as Nathan had declared he had so often done.

"Perhaps Nathan will help capture the fort," she thought. "Anyway he could show the Green Mountain Boys the way. If I were at home I would put a note in that cave near Lake Dunmore and tell Ethan Allen about Nathan."

Only Ethan Allen and a few of his friends knew of this mountain cave, and it was there messages were left for him by the men of the Wilderness.

CHAPTER XVI

LOUISE DISAPPEARS

THE guests for the quilting party arrived at an early hour in the afternoon. All that morning Faith and Aunt Prissy were busy. Dishes filled with red apples were brought up from the cellar; cakes were made ready, and the house in order before dinner time.

Only one little girl, Jane Tuttle, had been asked to come in the early afternoon. Jane was about Faith's age, and at school they were in the same classes. She was not very tall, and was very fat. Jane was one of the children whom Caroline and Catherine Young had taken especial delight in teasing.

> "Jane, Jane! Fat and plain;
> With a button nose and turned-in toes,"

they would call after her, until the little girl dreaded the very sight of them. When Faith had proved that she was not afraid of the sisters Jane Tuttle became her steadfast admirer, and was greatly pleased to come in the afternoon with her mother. But she was surprised to find Louise Trent there before her, and evidently very much at home. However, she was too kind-hearted a child not to be pleasant and polite to the lame girl, and Louise was now as ready to make friends as, before knowing Faith, she had been sullen and unfriendly.

Each of the girls was encouraged to set a few neat stitches in the quilt. Then, on the arrival of Mrs. Fairbanks and Mrs. Lewis, Aunt Prissy told Faith that if she wanted to take the little girls to her own room she might do so.

There was a glowing fire on the hearth, and Faith was pleased for Jane to see her pleasant chamber, and to introduce "Lady Amy."

"I wish I had brought my doll," said Jane, as the little girls gathered in front of the fire. "Mine is one my mother made for me."

"There, Louise! We could make you a doll!" exclaimed Faith, knowing how much her friend had always wished for a doll of her own.

But Louise shook her head. "I guess I am too old for dolls; I'm twelve," she said slowly, "and I don't have time to make dresses for dolls now that I'm learning to read and write. You see," and she turned to Jane, "I keep house for my father."

Jane looked at Louise, wondering to herself why she had ever imagined that Louise Trent was a girl that she could not have for a friend. Why, Louise was really pretty! thought fat little Jane, looking admiringly at the smooth black hair, and the neat and pretty dress. And so nearly grown-up, too. Twelve years old! Jane resolved to go and see Louise, and to ask her to come for a visit.

"I shall always play with dolls," she heard Faith declare. "I'd like to have a regiment of dolls, and play games with them. Wouldn't it be fun to have dolls that we could make up names for, and then have them do all sorts of things?"

Louise and Jane agreed that would be a fine game.

"We could dress up the pillows on your bed for dolls," suggested Louise.

"Yes, and put my dresses on them," responded Faith eagerly, running to the closet and bringing out the blue dress, a skirt and a small shawl. It was not long before two "cushiony" figures, as large as Jane, were seated on the bed.

"Let's put our coats and caps on them, Faith; and when the other girls come this evening we'll make them think the pillows are company," suggested Louise.

Jane jumped about the room with delight as Faith and Louise adjusted the caps and fur coats.

"We'll introduce them as Annie Snow and Mary White," said Faith. "It will be fun to see what the girls will say."

Four little girls were expected, and several boy friends of Donald's. Aunt Prissy wondered a little at Faith's eagerness to take the girls directly up-stairs on their arrival, but she was greatly pleased to see that Louise, Jane and Faith were evidently having a delightful time.

It was nearly dusk when the little visitors arrived, and Faith's room was rather dim and shadowy. The little girls coming in were rather surprised to find that there were strangers, evidently just arrived, sitting on Faith's bed.

"Girls, these are two of my best friends, Annie Snow and Mary White," said Faith, trying hard not to laugh, as her schoolmates bowed politely and greeted the stout figures on the bed, who, apparently, did not hear the introductions.

Jane, giggling with delight, circled around the newcomers; while Louise seated herself on the bed and began talking to Annie Snow. Faith endeavored to make the newcomers at ease, and it was not long before she had to run down-stairs to help her aunt with the supper, leaving Louise and Jane to carry on the game.

The children were to have their supper in the kitchen. The tables for young and old had been spread before the arrival of any of the guests, so there was but little for Aunt Prissy and Faith to do before calling the guests to supper.

Louise was the last one to enter the kitchen, her face radiant with fun and delight at the success of "Annie Snow" and "Mary White." She found a chance to tell Faith that "Annie" and "Mary" had managed to say that they didn't feel like eating supper, and that the girls had not yet discovered the joke.

"We'll bring them down after supper," Faith whispered.

"Are your friends from the Wilderness?" asked Peggy Tibbetts, the oldest girl of the party, as Faith sat down beside her.

"No," Faith answered slowly. "They are both coming down after supper, and I know you will be surprised when I tell you that they live right in this house."

Peggy Tibbetts was surprised. She looked almost frightened, and lost no time in whispering this information to the other girls; so that when Faith announced that she would run upstairs and ask "Annie" and "Mary" to come down there was an anxious silence.

Faith asked Jane to go with her, and in a few moments they returned with the two clumsy "girls." In the brightly-lit kitchen the dressed-up figures could no longer be mistaken, and the children were greatly pleased and amused by "Annie" and "Mary," who were established in straight-backed chairs, and urged to share in the supper.

There was so much laughter and merriment in the kitchen that Aunt Prissy looked in for a moment. "Faithie dear, who are the little girls in the corner?" she asked. To Louise and Jane this seemed a triumph indeed, and when Aunt Prissy, entering into the spirit of the affair, insisted upon being introduced to "Annie" and "Mary," and said she was very glad to see them, the children danced about, greatly pleased with this unexpected fun.

When the clock struck nine the grown people and children were all ready to start for home. Louise was to stay all night with Faith. As the children said their good-byes and stepped out into the snow-trodden path they called back messages to "Annie" and "Mary." The full moon shone down so brightly that the path could be plainly seen, and in the distance the dark line of the forest, and the heights of Ticonderoga.

"It's the best time I ever had in all my life," declared Jane, as she trotted off holding fast to her mother's hand.

And Faith said the same as she bade Aunt Prissy good-night. "It's fun to have parties, isn't it, Aunt Prissy," she said, "and all the girls are so pleasant."

"That is what makes the good time, isn't it?" responded her aunt.

"I hope it won't storm to-morrow," Louise said, as the two girls prepared for bed.

"What makes you think of a storm?" questioned Faith.

"There was a ring around the moon," said Louise; "that's one sign, and the air felt like snow."

But Faith was too happy over the evening to think about weather signs. She had, for that night, quite forgotten about the English soldiers and her resolve to send a message to Ethan Allen.

Louise's predictions proved right; for when the morning came snow was falling steadily, and great drifts were heaped up against the walls and fences. A chill east wind came sweeping across the ice-bound lake, and it was plain that there would be no more skating for many days.

For nearly a week trails and roads were impassable. Mr. Trent, knowing that Louise was safe and happy with her friends, made no effort to reach her; and the Scotts were glad to keep indoors, safe from the fierce cold and wind.

Donald and Hugh dug a tunnel to the shop, and Mr. Scott kept a path open to the barn, while indoors Aunt Prissy kept the two girls busy and happy. She declared that she had been hoping for a day to dye some recently woven blankets, and asked Faith what color she thought would be best.

"But how can you make any color you like, Aunt Prissy?" asked Faith.

"Perhaps not 'any color I like,' but I have a good lot of colors to choose from," replied Aunt Prissy. "People who live in the wilderness need only to step outdoors to find almost anywhere some plant that furnishes dye, and I gather my dye plants and roots every summer, as I am sure your own mother does."

"I know mother always gathers the dogwood roots to make a scarlet dye. Kashaqua told her about that," answered Faith. "The Indians use it for their feathers."

"And I am sure your mother dyed your brown dress with the shells of the hickory-nut," said Aunt Prissy, "and the yellow root is what I used to color the covers on the chair cushions in your room."

This was all new to Louise, and she listened eagerly, thinking to herself that she would color the faded quilts on her own bed; and that another summer she would gather a good supply of the roots and plants of which Mrs. Scott spoke.

"The pokeweed berries will color a good red," continued Mrs. Scott; "but for scarlet we must use the dogwood roots."

Then Mrs. Scott showed the little girls her bundles of dyestuffs, each plant and root tied up and marked carefully with its name and use. A large number of the dogwood roots were put into a huge iron kettle, the kettle filled with water, and hung over the fire. When it had boiled for several hours there would be a good scarlet dye in which the new blankets would be dipped. Then they would be hung to dry in the shed.

The next day the sun came out and shone brightly down on a white and glistening world, and that afternoon Mr. Trent came to take Louise home. He would not come in, but waited at the door until she was ready to go. But he thanked Mrs. Scott for all her kindness to his little daughter.

Faith was quite sure that Mr. Trent must be sorry to be a Tory instead of a loyal American. "But I suppose he can't help it," she decided, and always thought of her friend's father as unfortunate.

Faith and Louise always had so many things to talk about that they seldom spoke of the redcoats; and when they did Louise seemed to dislike them more than Faith herself.

Faith and Donald both had snow-shoes, and on their way to school, a few days later, Faith stopped at the shoemaker's door. But there was no response to her knock, and when she tried the door it would not open. She wondered where Louise and her father could be, but not until the next day did she hear that

the shoemaker and Louise had left their home,
apparently not to return. They had gone with a number of English families, on sledges, down the river,
without a good-bye to the kind friends who had
grown to love the little lame girl.

"I know Louise couldn't help it," Faith declared,
when Aunt Prissy told her the news. "She will write
to me, I know she will," but it was a long time before
any word came to her from her little friend. And now
Faith became more and more eager for March to
come, that she might once more see her father and
mother, and make some attempt to send a message
to Ethan Allen.

CHAPTER XVII

FAITH AGAIN VISITS THE FORT

THE night after hearing that Louise had gone Faith felt more nearly homesick than at any time since her arrival at her aunt's house. Everything seemed to remind her of her friend. Even "Lady Amy" made her remember that Louise had never owned a doll of her own.

"And I had meant to give Louise one of my strings of blue beads just as soon as I had asked Aunt Prissy," she thought, regretfully, holding up the pretty beads, and recalling how much Louise had admired them.

"Aunt Prissy," she called, running down the stairs and into the sitting-room, "may I not give Louise one of my bead necklaces?"

Aunt Prissy looked up in amazement.

"But how can you, Faithie, dear? We do not know where she is," she answered.

"We shall know some time. Of course we shall. And when we do, may I? I meant to ask you the day of the quilting," said Faith.

"Of course you may, child. I was sure that you would want to when Esther sent the beads. I only

151

hope you may have a chance to give them to Louise at an early day," responded Aunt Prissy.

This decision proved a comfort to Faith. As the weeks went by, and no news of the shoemaker and his little daughter was received, she would often look at the string of blue beads which she meant to give her friend. "I wish I had given them to her on my birthday," she thought regretfully, "but she shall have them some time," for Faith was quite sure that it could not be very long before Louise would find a way to let them know where she was.

March came, "stirring the fire" vigorously from the day of its arrival. The ice in the lake broke up rapidly, the snow melted, and by the middle of the month Faith began to expect her father. Nathan Beaman, in his clumsy boat, had crossed from Shoreham a number of times. He often teasingly reminded Faith of her plan to ask Ethan Allen to come and take possession of Fort Ticonderoga.

"You'd better hurry. The British will be sending men down from Canada by early summer, and then 'twill be of no use for the Green Mountain Boys to try to capture the fort," he said.

"How do you always know so much about what the English are going to do?" asked Faith.

The children were all in the shop. Nathan was helping Donald in the construction of a small boat, and

Faith and the two younger boys had been filling a basket with chips and shavings to carry into the house.

"Can't help knowing," answered Nathan. "I hear the men at the fort talking about all their fine plans to own all this country every time I go there."

"Nathan," and Faith lowered her voice so that the other children would not hear, "you know I promised not to tell about the door at the fort?"

Nathan nodded; he was looking at her sharply, and half feared that she was about to tell him that she had broken the promise.

"Well, of course I shan't tell. But if my telling some American would help send the soldiers away, mayn't I tell then?" and Faith's face was very serious as she waited for his response.

"Yes. I meant you weren't to tell Louise Trent, or those Young girls," said Nathan. "And don't tell any one unless you are sure it will be of some use. You see I may tell, if it comes to that."

Faith drew a long breath. "Thank you, Nathan," she said, in so serious a tone that the boy laughed aloud.

"You are as grave about that old fort as my father and the Shoreham men are. You ought to hear my father tell about the big fight here in 1758. He was a young man then, and the French held the fort, and the English were after it."

Donald had stopped his work, and he and Hugh were listening eagerly. "Tell us, tell us about it," said Donald.

"Father says there'll never be anything like it again. All the Colonies sent men, and Lord Howe brought thousands of English soldiers. England was our friend then," said Nathan. "They had thousands of boats, and rafts to carry their big guns. They had big flags, and music; and they didn't lurk or skulk about. Their boats came right down the lake in fine shape; they landed, and marched toward the fort. But the French were ready for them, and beat them back. However, the next year the English and Americans drove the French out."

"I guess the English are brave," Donald ventured, returning to his work.

"Of course they are. Why, we're all English ourselves," declared Nathan, "and that's why we won't stand being treated so unfairly. We can't stand it."

"I'm not English. I'm an American," said Faith; "and when the Americans take Ticonderoga that will be American too."

"That's the way to talk, little maid," said a gruff voice, and the children turned quickly toward the door.

"I didn't mean to listen," and a tall man, dressed in deerskin jacket and trousers, with moccasins, and wearing a fur cap, stepped into the shop, resting his musket against the wall near the door. "Shouldn't have dared come in if I had not heard I was in good company," he said laughingly, his sharp eyes looking carefully about the shop.

Nathan, with a half-muttered word of goodbye to the children, had started toward the door; but the newcomer's hand grasped his arm.

"Wait a minute!" he said, swinging the boy about. "I'm not so sure about letting you start off so smart. You may head straight for the fort, for all I know. What's your name?"

Nathan stood silent. His face flushed, but he looked the newcomer steadily in the face.

"Let go of Nathan!" said Donald sturdily, clutching at the man's arm, and kicking at his legs. "This isn't your shop. You let go of him."

"I guess I'd better," laughed the man, taking a firm hold of Donald and looking at both his captives in evident amusement. "Well, Philip Scott, what sort of a hornet's nest have you here?" he called out, and Faith turned around to see her Uncle Philip standing in the doorway. "I'll not let go these men until you promise to defend me," continued the stranger.

"You are safe, Phelps," responded Mr. Scott, coming forward and, as Nathan and Donald were released, giving the stranger a cordial welcome. Nathan vanished without a word, but on Mr. Scott's saying that he was the son of Mr. Beaman of Shoreham, the stranger was reassured. It was evident he did not wish his arrival to become known at the fort.

Faith heard the stranger say that he had come from Hartford, and that he would cross to the New Hampshire Grants as soon as he could safely do so.

"I'd like to look in at Fort Ticonderoga if I could without the soldiers knowing it," she heard him say, and her uncle replied that it would be impossible.

Faith was sure that this stranger was on some errand to the Green Mountain Boys, for he spoke of Remember Baker, and Seth Warner.

"I'd like to take Colonel Allen a plan of the fort," she heard him say, as she helped Aunt Prissy prepare an early dinner for their visitor.

Faith wished that she was grown up. Then, she was sure, she would dare to tell this stranger of the way up the cliff to the unguarded entrance. "He could go up this evening, and then he could tell Colonel Allen all about it," she thought, and before dinner was over she had resolved to find a way to tell him. But after a talk with Mr. Scott the visitor had declared he must get a few hours sleep. He said that he had been on the trail since very early that morning, and must be off again soon after sunset.

"Run in the sitting-room, Faithie, and fix a cushion for Mr. Phelps," said Aunt Prissy, and the little girl started obediently.

"I'll tell him now," she resolved, and as the tall man followed her she said quickly: "I know how you can get into the fort and no one see you. It's a secret. I'll show you. But Uncle Phil won't let me if you tell him."

"I'll not tell him. You are a brave child. Tell me quickly," responded the tall stranger.

"There's a canoe under the big willow at the bottom of the field—" began Faith, but he interrupted.

"Yes! Yes! I know. I am to cross the lake in it. But how can I get into the fort?"

"I could show you. I can't tell you," answered Faith.

"Then 'tis of small use. Harm might come to you, child," he answered, stretching himself out on the long settle with a tired sigh.

Faith went slowly back to the kitchen. Here was the very chance she had so long hoped for, and this stranger would not let her attempt it.

All that afternoon Faith was very quiet. She walked across the fields to the shore and looked at the big willow tree where the canoe was concealed. She looked off toward Mount Defiance, and Mount Hope, rising clearly against the sky, as if standing sentinels for Fort Ticonderoga.

"I'll try, anyway," she said to herself, as she turned toward home.

After supper she went early up-stairs. But she did not undress. She knew that her uncle would not go to the lake shore with his visitor, for that might attract the attention of some hunter or fisherman. It would not be long before Mr. Phelps would start. There was no time to lose. She put on her fur cap, and a knit jacket, and then peered out of the window. The sky was clear, and the moon made it almost as light as day. The sound of the falls came clearly through the quiet air.

"He could find his way up the cliff as plainly as if it were daylight," thought Faith, as she turned from the window.

She opened her door and closed it silently behind her. Her cousins were in bed, her uncle and aunt in the sitting-room with their visitor. Faith would have to pass the sitting-room door and go through the kitchen; the slightest noise would betray her. She had put on her moccasins, the ones Kashaqua had given her, and she stepped cautiously, without a sound. In a few moments she was safely out-of-doors and running across the field. She crouched down in the canoe and waited.

Faith did not hear or see the stranger as he came toward the shore—not until he grasped the canoe to push it into the water.

"King of Britain!" he whispered under his breath, when Faith spoke his name. "What are you doing here?"

"I'm going to show you the way into the fort. Yes! 'Twill take not more than an hour or two. Then you can leave me here. 'Twill do me no harm, and you will tell Colonel Allen about the fort," said Faith, in a whisper.

The man slid the canoe into the water. "You are well-named, Faith," he responded. "Well, 'tis a chance, and no man will harm a little maid," and with a stroke of his paddle he sent the canoe clear of the willows and headed toward the fort.

"Keep close to the shore," whispered Faith, peering anxiously ahead.

Several hours later Faith stepped from the canoe, and said a whispered good-bye to the stranger, and watched the canoe dart off straight toward Shoreham. He had scaled the cliff, while Faith kept the canoe close under the alder bushes, entered the door of the fort, and skilfully made his way about the fortifications, determining the right place for an attack and assuring himself that the fortress contained valuable stores.

As Faith stepped from the canoe the man tried to thank her.

"Some day your Uncle Scott will hear of this, and be proud indeed of so brave a child," he said, "and I shall tell Colonel Allen your name, and of your courage. Be sure of that. You have helped the American cause more than a regiment of soldiers."

Faith said over his words as she made her way across the fields. She recalled her first visit to the fort. "I'm glad those girls ran off that day," she thought, as she gently tried the back door. It was securely fastened. A low warning growl from "Scotchie" made her fear to lift a window. He would arouse the household. She stood on the steps, shivering a little in the sharp March wind. "I must get in without making a noise," she thought. But she could think of no way to accomplish it.

In spite of her silence "Scotchie" realized that some one was outside. He barked, growled, and once or twice threw himself against the door. Then suddenly his growls stopped, and, before Faith had time to move, the kitchen door opened slightly and she heard her uncle say, "Who's there?" and knew that, musket in hand, he was awaiting her answer.

CHAPTER XVIII

HOME AGAIN

"SCOTCHIE'S" warning growl turned to a joyful greeting as Faith spoke his name.

"Great Caesar! Faith!" exclaimed her uncle, drawing her into the kitchen. "What on earth are you doing out-of-doors at this time of night?"

"You locked the door," whimpered Faith.

"But why did you not call out? We thought you went straight to bed," said her uncle.

"I went down to the shore—" began Faith, and then stopped suddenly.

"Well, go straight to bed, and tell your aunt about it in the morning. She is fast asleep now."

Faith was glad to obey. She was too tired and sleepy to be greatly troubled by what would happen in the morning. She had resolved that if Aunt Prissy questioned her she would tell the truth. But she hoped earnestly that in some way the secret could be kept even from her aunt and uncle, until Mr. Phelps should tell them.

When she came down to breakfast it appeared that her uncle had only told Aunt Prissy that Faith had run out after supper, and, instead of calling and knocking until some one opened the door, had waited until "Scotchie's" bark had brought him to the door.

Aunt Prissy was more surprised and alarmed at this news than Faith had expected. She cautioned Faith never to go out without telling some one of the family.

"Why, some wolf or wildcat might have been about; or a party of Indians might have happened along and taken you off," she said. "And we should never have known what had become of you."

Faith promised never again to leave the house without her aunt's permission, and was glad indeed that she had escaped without telling of her journey to the fort.

"Aunt Prissy! Do you know what day this is?" she asked, so soberly that her aunt looked at her a little anxiously. "It is the very last day of March; it has been a warm and pleasant month, and my father has not come for me."

"And are you so anxious to say good-bye to us, Faithie? You know that instead of your making a visit home your father has decided it is best for you to stay; not come back unless for a visit, until another autumn," responded Aunt Prissy.

"Yes, I know. But why does he not come?" persisted Faith.

"Perhaps to-day will bring him," Aunt Prissy answered hopefully.

Faith came and stood close beside Aunt Prissy's chair. She wanted to say that she loved her cousins and uncle and Aunt Prissy very dearly; to tell her that she had been happy; and that it had been a beautiful visit; but that now she wanted to see her own dear mother more than anything else. But how could she say all this so that Aunt Prissy would understand?

Aunt Prissy put down her knitting and drew the little girl into her lap.

"There! Now tell me all about it, dear," she said, resting her face against Faith's yellow curls.

And Faith told her all that she had been thinking; all that she had thought would be so difficult. And Aunt Prissy listened, saying, "Of course," and "Yes, indeed," from time to time, and understanding even more than Faith found words to tell.

"Why, Aunt Prissy, it's almost like having two homes," concluded Faith.

Before Aunt Prissy could answer there was the sound of voices in the kitchen, and Donald, closely followed by Mr. Carew, came into the room.

"It's the very last day of March!" Faith reminded him.

"And I came near not getting here to-day," her father replied, as Faith drew him to the big chair near the window, and climbed to a seat on his knees. "I was held up on the trail by a tall fellow,

from Connecticut, as it proved. He was bound to
make me own up that I was an English spy. I told
him my name, and my errand, and when I spoke
Faith's name, why, he was at once my best friend,
told me of his visit at this house, and could not say
enough in praise of my little daughter," responded
Mr. Carew.

"The Americans seem to be gaining courage," said
Aunt Prissy. "The men of the Wilderness do not mean
to let the other Colonies do all the fighting, I'm sure."

"Indeed we'll do our part, Priscilla," her brother
assured her.

Faith told her father of the disappearance of Mr.
Trent and Louise; of the quilting party, and of all the
happenings since his November visit. But she did not
tell him of guiding the Connecticut man to the path-
way up the cliff to Fort Ticonderoga.

It was evident that Mr. Phelps had kept the secret
for some purpose of his own; so, much as she wanted
her father to know, Faith resolved that she would not
tell him. This secret did not worry and trouble her as
the others had done. "I guess it's because this secret
means helping somebody, and the others were just—
well, just mean secrets," Faith decided, as she
thought it over.

The next morning Faith and her father were ready
to start at an early hour. Uncle Phil, Aunt Prissy,

the boys and "Scotchie" walked with them to the shore.

"You will come back when summer comes, won't you, Cousin Faith?" said Donald. "You'll come for a visit even if you don't stay and go to school."

"I will if I can," Faith promised, "and when Louise comes back give her the blue beads, Aunt Prissy."

"Yes, indeed, dear child," responded her aunt, wondering to herself if Louise and her father would ever again be seen in that vicinity. Then there were messages for Faith's mother, and not until she was in the canoe were the good-byes really said.

The little group stood on the shore watching the canoe for some minutes, and then turned back toward the house. They were all very quiet, but as they reached the road Donald called out: "There's somebody on our door-step! Why, it is Louise! Yes, it is," and with a gay call he was off, running swiftly toward the house while the others hurried after him.

"Where is Faith?" Louise asked eagerly, when Mrs. Scott had welcomed her, and they were in the big kitchen.

"She's gone home," said Donald, before his mother could answer. But Mrs. Scott told the little girl of how much Faith had missed her, and of the string of blue beads that she had left to be given to Louise.

It was evident that Louise was greatly disappointed to find that her friend had gone. But she fastened the beads about her neck, and touched them with loving fingers.

"Faith was my very first friend," she said. "My father says that we have come back to stay," she added, "and perhaps Faith will come in the summer?" There was such a pleading, questioning look in the girl's dark eyes that Mrs. Scott felt a new tenderness and sympathy for her, and put her arm about Louise as she answered:

"Perhaps she will. But you must come often and see me; for we shall both miss her very much."

"Oh, may I, Mrs. Scott? I was afraid you wouldn't want me to come," and Louise's face brightened.

"Why, I am to help you with your studies, and Donald is to call for you when you begin school. Faith arranged all that," responded Mrs. Scott smilingly.

Faith was silent as the canoe went swiftly across the lake, and they had nearly reached the shore before she began asking questions about "Bounce," whom her father declared to be now a "grown-up cat," and about all the familiar things about the house and mill.

"Listen, father!" she said, as they landed, and he drew the canoe to its hiding-place in the alder bushes. "Hear the falls!" and for a moment the two stood quietly hearkening to the "Chiming Waters."

Then Mr. Carew adjusted the pack, containing Faith's belongings, picked up his musket, without which no woodsman dared travel in those days, and they started up the trail.

Everywhere were evidences that spring was near at hand. Many trees and shrubs were showing the delicate gray green of coming buds; and now and then the fragrance of the wild arbutus was in the air. Birds were busy; woodthrushes and pewees were calling; now and then a golden-throated warbler sounded his clear note. The air was soft and warm for the season, and Faith was so happy in the thought of being really on her way home that she forgot for a time that Mr. Phelps had said that no American settler's home in the Wilderness could be safe until Fort Ticonderoga was held by American soldiers.

"It's lovely to be going home, isn't it, father?" she said and Mr. Carew smiled down at his little daughter, and agreed with her that nothing better could be desired.

> " We shall see with glad surprise
> Lilies spring, and verdure rise;
> And soon, amidst the wilds, we'll hear
> Murmuring waters falling clear,"—

sang Mr. Carew softly.

"Oh, that is mother's song," exclaimed Faith. "It just means home, doesn't it?" And again her father was quite ready to agree.

They walked slowly up the rocky trail and when they reached the top of the first ridge they stopped to rest and eat the excellent lunch that Aunt Prissy had prepared for them. But Faith declared that she was not tired. It seemed to her that she could run all the way if her father would only permit. And when in the early afternoon she first heard the sound of the mill-stream she did run, until, out of breath, she had to rest on a moss-grown stump for her father to catch up with her.

And then, in a short time, they were standing on the edge of the clearing. The brook was dancing and singing as if eager to welcome Faith; the sun shone warmly down on mill and cabin and running down the path came Mrs. Carew; while standing near the cabin was Kashaqua, in her gayest feathers, grunting and smiling.

"Mother dear! Mother dear!" called Faith, as she ran forward and was held close in her mother's arms.

CHAPTER XIX

FAITH WRITES A LETTER

KASHAQUA was evidently delighted to see Faith safely at home once more. She had brought a present for her little friend; and after Faith had talked to her mother, and yet, as she declared, had "not begun to tell her" all she had to tell, Kashaqua unrolled a soft bundle and spread out the skin of a black bear cub. It was hardly larger than the skin of a good-sized puppy; but the fur was so soft and glossy that Faith and her mother exclaimed admiringly over its beauty, and Faith said that she would take the greatest care of it. She questioned Kashaqua about "Nooski," the tame bear which had followed them on their journey to Ticonderoga.

"Gone!" replied Kashaqua, and had no more to tell of the wild creature that she had tamed, and, suddenly, Kashaqua disappeared in her usual silent fashion without a sign or word of farewell.

Faith was tired, and quite satisfied to rest on the big settle and talk to her mother, while "Bounce," steady and well-behaved, curled up on the hearth rug. Faith told her mother about Louise; about Caroline and Catherine and their mischief, and of the quilting party. She told her about Nathan Beaman, and of the skating on the lake, and how the English soldiers had extinguished the fire and spoiled their fun. But she did not tell her of the evening when she had guided Mr. Phelps up the moonlit lake to the foot of the cliffs, and told him how to make his way into the fort. Some time, she resolved, her mother should know all about it; but she still felt that she must keep it a secret.

Mrs. Carew asked many questions about the fort.

"There is more travel over the trails than ever before," she told the little girl, "and we hardly know who are our friends. The English are sending their spies everywhere. Be very cautious, Faithie, and say nothing to any stranger that you have ever been near Fort Ticonderoga. This part of the country will not be safe until American soldiers take the place of the English in the fort."

"Oh, mother dear, I hope they will soon. I wish that I could help take the fort."

"Who knows but you may help in some way, when the right time comes," her mother responded, smiling at her little daughter's eagerness. "Now, I am going out to get something for you.

Something that you will like very much," she added, and left Faith alone.

Faith closed her eyes, wondering happily what it was that her mother would bring. She thought of the caraway cookies, of the little round pies made of the dried pumpkin, and then a noise at the door made her open her eyes. For an instant she believed that she must be asleep and dreaming, for Esther Eldridge was standing in the door—Esther grown taller and stronger, with red cheeks and shining eyes.

"Yes, it's really Esther," Mrs. Carew called over the little girl's shoulder, and Esther ran toward the settle as Faith started forward to meet her.

"Isn't this a fine surprise?" Esther exclaimed. "I was so afraid you would hear about our living here before you got home."

"Living here?" questioned Faith, looking so puzzled that both Mrs. Carew and Esther laughed aloud.

"Yes! yes, indeed! My father and mother and I," answered Esther delightedly.

"But where? I have been up-stairs, and all over the house and I didn't see anybody, or anything," said Faith.

"Oh, we live in our own house—a house just like this; or it will be just like this when it is all finished," and Esther told of her father's decision to bring his family to the Wilderness to live. He had purchased a grant of land adjoining that held by Mr. Carew soon after Esther's visit in September. The timber for the cabin had been cut early in the winter, and the cabin begun, and now it was nearly finished. "We moved last week," said Esther, "and you can see our house from your back door."

Faith forgot all about being tired and ran to the back door to look. Yes, there it was; the big new cabin, near the path down which Ethan Allen had led her home, when, angry at Esther, she had run off to the woods.

"Isn't it splendid! Oh, Esther, it is the very best thing that ever happened," Faith declared; "isn't it, mother dear?"

Mrs. Carew was quite ready to agree with her little daughter. "Good neighbors was the only thing we really lacked," she agreed, "and perhaps others will come when there is better protection for their safety."

The two little friends had much to tell each other, and when Esther started for home Faith walked with her as far as the mill. From the mill the new cabin could be clearly seen.

"Do you remember asking me if I listened to the brook?" Esther asked laughingly, as they stood looking at the dancing waters of the stream. "Well, I know now just what you meant. It's company, isn't it?"

Then Faith told her of the "Chiming Waters" of Ticonderoga, and of some of the old tales of the lake that her aunt and Nathan had related.

"Did you see the English soldiers?" questioned Esther.

"Oh, yes." And Faith described the skating party on the lake that the redcoats had interfered with. "I wish I could see Ethan Allen, as I did that day in September, and tell him all about the fort and the soldiers, and ask him to drive the English away. My father says that Colonel Allen could drive them away," said Faith.

"Of course he could! My father says so, too," agreed Esther. "Would it not be a fine thing for us to send him a letter, Faith, and ask him?"

"Oh, Esther! That's just what I thought of." But we ought to do it right away, for more soldiers are coming to the fort, Nathan Beaman says, and then it won't be so easy," responded Faith.

The two little girls talked earnestly. They both knew of the cave on the rocky slope near Lake Dunmore, and that messages were sometimes left there for the settlers. But Lake Dunmore was a long distance away.

"It would take all day to go and get back," said Esther, "and our mothers would never let us go; you know they wouldn't."

"One of us ought to go to-morrow," answered Faith, "but how can we plan it?"

"I know! I know!" declared Esther. "I'll ask your mother if you may come for a visit, and then you'll go home at night. Some time you can tell her all about it," concluded Esther as she noticed Faith's serious and doubtful expression.

"And what will you do? Don't you mean to go with me?" asked Faith.

"Oh, yes! I'll tell my mother I am going to spend the day with you. Then we'll start off in good season, and we'll get home before our mothers miss us," said Esther.

"Faith! Faith!" and Mrs. Carew's voice sounded through the clear air.

"I must run back now. I'll write the letter to-night and be over near your house as early as I can in the morning," said Faith.

"Hide behind the big pine," said Esther, and the two friends, greatly excited over their project, separated and ran toward their respective homes.

It was not easy for Faith to write the letter, for she would have to ask her mother for the quill pen, and the bottle of ink, made from the juice of the pokeberry. But in the early evening, while her mother was busy, Faith secured the quill and ink and a sheet of the treasured paper and wrote her letter:

"Dear Mr. Colonel Ethan Allen," she wrote. "Will you please send the English soldiers away from Fort Ticonderoga? Nathan Beaman, who lives at Shoreham, will show you how to get in. Please send them soon, or more will come.

"Respectfully your friend,
"FAITH CAREW."

She had time to fold and seal the letter with the big stick of red wax, softening the wax before the sitting-room fire. A moment later and her mother came in, saying she had best go to bed and get a good night's rest.

"May I spend to-morrow, all day, with Esther?" asked Faith, as her mother went upstairs with her, and feeling her face flush with the consciousness of not telling her mother all the truth.

"Your very first day at home, dear child! Why, I should be running over to Mrs. Eldridge's every hour to make sure that you were really within reach," responded her mother.

"Oh, mother, you wouldn't!" said Faith, so earnestly that Mrs. Carew smiled reassuringly and said:

"Well, perhaps not every hour. But if you want to spend the day with Esther you may. 'Tis not as if you were going back to Aunt Prissy in a week."

"And you won't come to Mrs. Eldridge's at all, will you, mother dear?" pleaded Faith. "I'll be safe, and I'll come home early."

"You shall do as you like, dear child. I know you will do nothing but what will please me," and Mrs. Carew leaned over to kiss Faith good-night.

"Oh, dear," Faith whispered to herself guiltily, as her mother went down the stairs. "Here is another secret, the biggest of all. But I can't tell mother."

The song of the brook seemed louder than ever before to the little girl that night, as she lay watching the April stars shine through her window. She remembered that her mother had said that perhaps a little girl could help. "Mother dear is sure to be glad when she knows that Colonel Allen had to be told about Nathan," thought Faith; and then the brook's song grew softer and softer and she was fast asleep.

Faith was down-stairs the next morning almost as soon as her father and mother. She had on her brown dress and her moccasins, and the letter was safely hidden in her pocket. She could hardly keep still long enough to eat her breakfast.

"Esther wanted me to come early, mother dear, and I promised," she urged; so her mother bade her be off, and stood in the door and watched the little girl run down the slope, feeling a little disappointed that Faith should be so eager to be with Esther instead of remaining at home.

But early as it was Faith found Esther waiting for her.

"Did you bring anything to eat?" asked Esther.

"I never thought of it!" replied Faith, "and I don't believe I could, anyway."

"Well, I thought of it. I have a fine square of corn cake, a piece of cold venison, and a square of molasses cake," said Esther, holding up a small basket. "Now, creep along on the edge of the trail until we are well up the ridge. Then we can walk as we please."

Faith obeyed. She thought to herself how fortunate it was that Esther had come to live in the Wilderness, and that she was ready to help carry the message.

"Isn't it lovely in the woods!" said Esther, as they reached the summit of the ridge, and turned to look back down the winding trail. "Father said this morning that the spring was early, and 'tis surely warm as summer."

As they rested for a little while on a bank of firm green moss Faith told Esther of "Nooski's" sudden appearance when she and Kashaqua were on their journey to the lake.

"Goodness!" exclaimed Esther, peering anxiously into the underbrush. "I hope we shan't see any bears to-day, not even a tame one."

The sun was high in the April skies when the two little girls came in sight of Lake Dunmore. The trail led near the lake; and Esther was very sure that she knew just where to look for the cave.

"It's near a big pine tree, and you can only see rocks. Father showed me when we came from Brandon," she said.

The little girls were very tired and hungry, and Faith suggested that they should eat their luncheon and rest before searching for the cave.

"I wish I had brought more corn bread," said Esther, when they had finished the last morsel of the food.

"It's lucky you brought as much as you did," responded Faith. "We'd better begin looking for the cave now."

It was hard work climbing up the rocky hill-side, and it did not seem such an easy matter to locate the cave as Esther had expected. They peered under rocks, and climbed over ledges, and were nearly discouraged when a sudden noise made Faith grasp Esther's arm with a whispered "Hush"; for almost in front of them, apparently coming directly out of the hillside, appeared the head and shoulders of a man.

But they were too near to conceal themselves or to try and run away.

"Great Caesar's Ghost!" exclaimed the man, crawling out from the cave. "Two little maids! Where did you come from?"

Faith's hold on Esther's arm tightened. "Don't tell. Don't answer his questions," she whispered, remembering her mother's caution about strangers, and thinking perhaps this might be an English spy who had discovered the cave.

"Where are the others?" asked the man.

Esther looked questioningly at Faith, but neither of them spoke.

The man's stern face softened as he looked at the two little figures. He realized they must be the children of some settler in the Wilderness—perhaps children who had wandered too far from home and lost their way.

"You need not be afraid to speak," he said smilingly. "Perhaps I know your fathers. Tell me your names."

Faith was quite sure that this was a question which could be safely answered, so both the little girls spoke their names, and instantly the man responded by saying:

"Then you," and he nodded to Faith, "are Miller Carew's daughter. I know your father well. Tell him

Seth Warner has been in Salisbury and is now starting back to Bennington. But how come you this distance from home?"

Both Faith and Esther knew that Seth Warner was a friend of the settlers, and before he had finished speaking Faith was quite ready to tell him their errand and to give the note for Colonel Allen into his hands.

He listened in evident amazement to the story of their morning's journey, for he well knew the dangers of the wilderness trail.

"I will go with you to within sight of your homes," insisted their new friend, "and I shall not forget to tell Colonel Allen of your courage."

"Will he come soon and take the fort?" asked Faith.

"More quickly for your help than without it, little maid. But go not so far from home again," Mr. Warner answered, with a kindly smile.

It was sunset, and Mr. Carew was starting to bring Faith home from her visit to Esther, when he saw his little daughter coming down the path. She walked so slowly that her father hastened to meet her.

"I'm so tired, father," she said. "Couldn't you carry me home?"

"Of course I can," and he lifted her in his arms and, anxious and worried by her pale face and evident fatigue, hurried toward the house.

CHAPTER XX

THE CAPTURE OF THE FORT

IT was noon the next day when Faith awoke; and although she was quite ready to dress and go down-stairs, her mother thought it best for her to stay in bed.

Faith wondered to herself if Esther's feet ached as hers did; and, more than this, she was anxious to know if their parents had any idea of where she and Esther had spent the previous day.

"There will be so much for me to tell mother," she thought, a little uneasily, hoping that soon she would again have no secrets to conceal.

When Faith came down-stairs she found Esther waiting to see her; and, in response to Faith's questioning look, she nodded and smiled reassuringly. Esther had brought over her English grammar, for it had been decided that the two little girls were to study together two hours each day; one day at Faith's house, and the next at Esther's.

"It's all right; our mothers don't know. But what made you so tired?" said Esther, as soon as the girls were alone.

Faith shook her head. "I don't know. I do hope we can tell all about it soon. I've a great mind to tell mother now."

"You mustn't. Don't you remember? Mr. Warner said that soon he would tell our fathers, and they would be proud of us. But if we tell them now they won't be proud; they will be vexed, and maybe punish us. Wait until Colonel Allen tells them that you helped him. Then 'twill be all right," advised Esther, and Faith agreed, a little doubtfully.

It was difficult for the two little girls to fix their minds on their lessons that day, and for many days to come. They both watched the trail, each day expecting to see some messenger who would bring news that Colonel Allen was in possession of Fort Ticonderoga; but April passed, and Esther declared that she did not believe the Americans wanted the fort.

"I am going to tell my mother everything. All about our going to Lake Dunmore, and my letter, and something else," declared Faith.

It was one day early in May, and she and Esther were coming up from Beaver meadow, where they had been watching the little creatures, who were very active and did not seem to fear the two little figures at the edge of the woods. The beavers were building a dam; they had dragged trees to the side of the stream, and it seemed a very wonderful thing to

Esther when she saw the beavers sink one end of these stakes, while others raised and fastened the other end, twisting in the small branches of the trees, and plastering mud over all with their feet and tails. She was thinking to herself that there were more strange things to see in the Wilderness in one day than in a whole year in a village, when she felt Faith seize her arm and say laughingly:

"You haven't heard a word. Now, listen! I am going to tell my mother."

The little girls were now in sight of the clearing, and, before Esther could answer, Faith stopped suddenly and exclaimed:

"Look, Esther! There's a man just leaving the mill, and running up the trail as fast as he can go. A stranger."

Quite forgetting beavers and secrets the two little girls ran toward the house. "There's my father," said Esther as they reached the door.

Mr. and Mrs. Eldridge were both in the kitchen of the Carew house, and none of the elder people appeared to notice the two girls.

Mr. Carew was loading his musket, and Faith's mother was packing a knapsack with provisions.

"Here are the children," said Mrs. Eldridge, as she turned toward the door; and then Esther saw that her father was waiting for Mr. Carew.

"Faithie dear, your father is going to Castleton," said Mrs. Carew, fastening the knapsack, and in a moment Faith was held close in her father's arms, and then the two men were off striding down the trail.

"Are they going to take Ticonderoga?" Faith questioned eagerly.

The two women looked at her in surprise, but Mrs. Carew answered quickly:

"Of course they are. Americans are guarding the trail, so we are safe enough at present. But neither of you girls must go beyond the clearing."

"When shall we know about the fort, mother? When will we know?" asked Faith.

"Soon, I hope, child. But talk not of it now," responded her mother.

But after a little Mrs. Eldridge told them that a messenger had come from Bennington, summoning the settlers to Castleton to meet Colonel Allen. Faith and Esther listened to the story of the far-off battle of Lexington, in Massachusetts, the news of which had determined the Green Mountain Boys to make an immediate attack on the fort. These men were the settlers of the New Hampshire Grants, living long distances apart, and obliged to travel over rough trails, through deep forests, across rivers and mountains.

There were no smooth roads or fleet horses to help them on their way; there was little time for preparation when Allen's summons came; they had no uniforms, no strains of music; but no truer soldiers ever faced danger than the Green Mountain Boys.

That night Faith told her mother the story of her adventure in the fort, when Nathan had rescued her and taken her down the cliff. She told of the evening in March when she had guided Mr. Phelps along the moonlit shore of the lake and told him of the entrance to the fort; and last of all she described her journey with Esther over the trail to Lake Dunmore, and the letter to Ethan Allen which she had given to Seth Warner.

Mrs. Carew listened in amazement; but she had no word of blame for Faith. She realized the dangers the child had so unknowingly faced with a sense that her little girl had been guarded by a protection greater than any by which she could have surrounded her; and she wondered, too, if it were not possible that Faith might not really have helped in the great undertaking for which her father was ready to give all that he had to give.

"Mother dear, I despise secrets," Faith whispered, as she finished the story, "and I mean never to have another one."

Three days later Mr. Carew came swinging across the clearing. He waved his cap in the air as Faith came running to meet him.

"Ticonderoga is ours," he called, "and the English prisoners are on their way to Hartford. And so it was you, little maid, who helped Phelps to a plan of the fort, and told Ethan Allen of young Beaman!"

"Did it help, father? Did it help?" Faith asked eagerly.

"Help? Indeed it did. Young Beaman led the way to the fort, and we were in without firing a shot. And Colonel Allen and his men hold the fort," replied Mr. Carew.

He could stay for but a few hours, as he was carrying the news to the settlements. It was several days before he was at home again, and told them more fully of Allen's triumph, and of the capture of Crown Point by Seth Warner and his followers.

Toward the last of May Aunt Prissy, accompanied by Nathan Beaman, arrived at the log cabin, and Faith heard the story of Louise's arrival at Ticonderoga.

"Her father has been taken a prisoner to Hartford, and Louise will stay with me," Aunt Prissy said. "I will adopt her for my own daughter if her father consents."

"I do hope he will," said Faith, glad indeed to know that her friend was safe.

"And so my little Faith did help take the fort after all, thanks to Nathan," said Aunt Prissy, smiling down at her little niece.

" 'Twas Faith who really helped, for she told Colonel Allen about me," Nathan added handsomely.

All this made Faith a very happy little girl; but when, a few weeks later, a messenger brought her a letter from Ethan Allen himself, she felt that no other little girl in all the American Colonies could be as proud as Faith Carew. She confessed to her mother that, after all, some secrets were worth keeping. Colonel Allen invited her to make a visit to the fort, and it was arranged that her father should take her to Ticonderoga and that she should stay for a few days with Aunt Prissy.

So once again she went over the trail and crossed the lake, and on a pleasant June morning with her father and Aunt Prissy, she stood again at the entrance to Fort Ticonderoga. This time she was not left alone, as on her first visit, a frightened deserted child. For it was Colonel Allen himself, tall and handsome, who met the little party at the entrance and escorted them about the fortifications.

" 'Faith,' " he said kindly, as he bade them goodbye, " 'tis indeed the best of names for a little American girl; a name that I shall ever remember."

Faith was very quiet as they walked toward home. She was thinking to herself of all the happy experiences of the past weeks; and not until she saw Louise waiting for her at Aunt Prissy's gate did her face lose its serious expression. She ran ahead of the others and called out: "Louise! Louise! You will be Aunt Prissy's little girl, won't you? Because then you'll really be an American."

Louise nodded happily.

"Yes; and father is going to be an American, too. Didn't Aunt Prissy tell you?" she responded; "and it's all because you were my friend, Faith," she added more soberly, as the two girls entered the house, and stood hand in hand at the door where, but a few months ago, Louise had entered a ragged, unhappy child.

"We'll always be friends, shan't we!" said Faith, and Louise earnestly responded:

"Always."

The Stories in This Series Are:
A LITTLE MAID OF PROVINCETOWN
A LITTLE MAID OF MASSACHUSETTS COLONY
A LITTLE MAID OF NARRAGANSETT BAY
A LITTLE MAID OF OLD PHILADELPHIA
A LITTLE MAID OF OLD NEW YORK
A LITTLE MAID OF OLD CONNECTICUT
A LITTLE MAID OF TICONDEROGA
A LITTLE MAID OF VIRGINIA
A LITTLE MAID OF MARYLAND
A LITTLE MAID OF MOHAWK VALLEY
A LITTLE MAID OF OLD MAINE

Available from:
APPLEWOOD BOOKS
Bedford, MA 01730